In It To Win It

When Your Doctor Says, STAT!!!

Lynn Michelle Salyer

Footprint Publications

DEDICATION

This book is sincerely dedicated to Leisha, Luke, Tim, Ali, Momma, Pops, Sis, Brub, Mer, Crystal Lynn, Roles, Nate, Adam, Clay, Dre, Colty, Indy, Brody and the rest of my entire amazing family. I truly would not be here to tell this story without your love, support and strength, I love you all with my entire heart.

I also dedicate this project to all of my friends, too many to try to list, you all know who you are. Your unending support and encouragement helped get me where I am today and I cannot adequately express my thanks and love to each one of you.

This book would not have happened if it wasn't for David, he urged me to begin writing a blog. He set up the blog for me, got me started and I never looked back. The day that I text him and asked him to call me about this project, he said that he was just waiting on the appropriate day to text me and say, "When are you writing a book?" I am so grateful and indebted to you for the hours spent on this project, thank you from my heart.

Ultimately, everything I do is dedicated to the One who has truly brought me to this day in my life, my Heavenly Father, without Him I could do nothing. I am forever grateful to my Lord and Savior and I remain thankful every day that He is never surprised!

Philippians 4:13 - I can do ALL things through Him who strengthens me.

#inittowinit

FORWARD

Cancer happens. I hate that statement, but I have had to come to terms with that fact.

As you read this book, don't be fooled into believing that it is about cancer. It's not. This story is about a journey of love of family. It is a story of trust and of faith.

This narrative is one that can only be told through the perspective of my sister-in-law, Lynn Salyer.

It is said that, life waits for no-one. Food still needs to be purchased and prepared. Bills need to be paid. Mom's need to be moms. Activities go on, and life needs to be lived. Lynn takes us on a journey of life, family and faith.

After you read this book, you will see that cancer will never define who Lynn is. You will see Lynn, the athlete, who loves competition and never backs down from a challenge. You will see one of Ohio State's biggest fans. You will see a mom, dancing at her daughter's wedding, trying to be normal during the darkest stretch of chemotherapy. Most importantly, you will see someone who loves God, her family and her children more than life itself.

She shows us how to be in it, to win it… even when the doctor says, "STAT!!"

David Michael Lee

CONTENTS

ONE

THE ROAD TRIP

Ahhhh… Christmas time! I am equally as crazy about Christmas time as I am about The Ohio State Buckeyes football season. I have been a huge fan of both all of my life!

That being said, Christmas 2016 seemed to come even more quickly than normal and I just did not feel like myself at all, I did not have the energy that typically comes along with the enthusiasm I have for this particular season and holiday.

During the Christmas season, my daughter Leisha and her fiancé Tim had discussed going on a road trip with me in February, the best part of this discussion was the destination of this trip, Seymour, Tennessee! Since my children were born, our favorite place to vacation was east Tennessee… partly because of the mountains and mostly because of our family who lives there!

We scheduled it for mid-February in hopes that the winter weather would not prevent us from going. I was hoping that by that time I would be feeling better, as I mentioned before, I just had not felt "right" for quite some time.

Now, before any of you start reading this with the thoughts that I should have done something about the way I felt, let's rewind even more to April of 2016. I had not been feeling the greatest as early as the Spring, so I scheduled my yearly check-up, PAP test, and blood work, the whole deal! I went in for my appointment with Dr. Haynes, who is more like a friend than just a physician, and she asked me the typical questions and had my blood work results.

To my surprise, my blood work results were terrific; in fact, the nurses were cheering for me stating that my results were almost perfect and that for a forty-nine-year-old it was amazing, so just to keep doing what I was doing.

Dr. Haynes performed my PAP test and talked to me about my hiatal hernia which we assumed was causing my current digestive issues. She explained that due to my age I would probably start experiencing period changes and that pre-menopause should be approaching soon as well.

So, I left feeling better that I went, as well as feeling my age and realizing that this year would probably be a big year for me, turning the big 5-0 and possibly going through menopause!

That summer held many activities, heading up not one, but two-family reunions. At one of the reunions, Tim pulled off any amazing surprise proposal to Leisha. It was unforgettable! They set the wedding date for May 27, 2017, thus another reason that 2017 would be a BIG year for all of us!

Fall came quickly, along with it, my final year of coaching volleyball for Woodmore High School. I coached the JV team and assisted Leisha with the varsity girls. These girls and their families became so very special to us, we were not just a team, we were family. By the end of the volleyball season, I was so relieved to see it come to an end just because of my physical stamina, I kept losing a couple pounds here and there and just kept feeling more and more fatigued.

Thanksgiving arrived and with it all of the wonderful traditions we look forward to each year, including a large family get together at my Aunt Bonnie's home. I prepared a turkey and my annual home-made dressing to go with the bird.

Again, I did not enjoy the activities as much as normal because of my health, in addition to the fatigue factor I had also realized that almost everything I ate disturbed my stomach and I basically ate enough to survive because I always felt very "full." I noticed that I was taking Tums much more than in the past, as well.

While we attended the Thanksgiving dinner, my cousin Jayne (who is a nurse) made me promise I would see my family physician because I looked "sick". I made my appointment for the Tuesday after the holiday.

Upon my arrival to see my doc, Dr. Haynes thought I looked thinner than when I had visited her in April and she also informed me that my PAP test in April came back slightly abnormal, so we needed to repeat it at this appointment. We also discussed my digestive issues, she was very inquisitive as to where the discomfort was and I insisted that it was all in my upper abdomen, nothing down low. We adjusted my diet and she told me that if I did not feel better in a couple weeks to get ahold of her and she would prescribe something for my hiatal hernia symptoms.

On December 7th, my Mom had a stroke, my Pops called an ambulance and they took her to Toledo Hospital. This was the third stroke she had endured within a few months span. We all went up to the hospital and I remember talking to my sister Pam about Mom and then telling her that I had not been feeling well myself and about my doctor's appointments.

Remarkably, I noticed that day at the hospital that I felt better than I had in a long time, this was encouraging to me! Mom recouped well from her stroke and we were so grateful as Christmas was approaching so quickly.

Throughout the holidays I did not have my typical energy, but it was Christmas, everyone feels better at Christmas time! The family was together and I enjoyed each second of it as much as I could with not feeling the best.

So…. here we are, back at the beginning, planning our road trip to Tennessee! As February progressed I noticed an atypical bloating going on in my stomach. At first the bloat would go away while I slept at night, then go down by the next morning.

After a couple of weeks though, the bloat just stayed and it caused so much pain and tightness that I dreaded even trying to roll out of bed in the mornings. By the time of our weekend trip to Tennessee I was feeling completely miserable! Tim and Leisha needed to take care of some wedding business on this trip, so I knew in my mind that I needed to accompany them to Tennessee and then get to the bottom of my health situation when we returned.

Typically, I will use any excuse to get to the Smokies, I love the mountains and the family and friends that I have there are priceless! The purpose of the trip was for Tim and Leisha to get pre-marriage counseling from my cousin Aaron who would be officiating their wedding in May.

The same cousin had a baby boy on December 31st and we could not wait to meet little Ridge, as well. So, with all of this in mind, how could I possibly be dreading this trip? Why did I want to postpone or even cancel it? What was wrong with me? Looking back, I realize that physically I was so sick, but I felt like this time away in such a magical place might be the "medication" that could fix me right up!

Friday, February 17th rolled around, the day of our big trip! We decided to leave that night after work, so we knew that the eight-hour drive would seem even longer than usual because of when we left. I

4

decided that if I was going to be in the car anyway I might as well drive. Typically, I love to drive and I thought it would be a good distraction for how I felt.

We had decided to stop off in Grove City for a quick visit with some very good friends and to grab some dinner. We did that and I was so glad to get to rest for a bit. Everyone enjoyed the dinner except for me, I was afraid to put very much into my sore and distended stomach.

After we left our friends, I entertained the idea of stopping off at my brother's home in Kentucky, it would be a much-needed rest stop for me to break up the trip and we always adore any time we get to spend with Eric, his wife Meredith and my nephew, Colton.

We made the executive decision to stop there and we had a wonderful visit with them, I did not mention my stomach or the way I was feeling. (Looking back, I realize that I did not mention it because I really did not want to worry anyone) We spent the night with them and then headed out the next morning bright and early to finish the last leg of our trip. In the back of my mind I was hoping and praying that somehow I would breathe that Tennessee Mountain air and POOF, feel better! ☺

We had a terrific time with uncles, aunts, cousins, friends and of course the new little bundle of joy, Ridge, it was definitely just what the doctor would have ordered… I thought.

Unfortunately, my sickness did not let up, in fact, on Saturday I spent a great deal of time in the bathroom, I was indeed, miserable. We stayed until Monday morning and had to head out on our long journey home. I would be misleading if I did not add here that I was dreading the drive home worse than I had the drive there!

Thankfully, it was an uneventful trip. I was never so happy to get out of the car and get to my parent's home, all I wanted was Mom's pink rice bag heated and placed on my feet. This rice bag had become my best friend throughout the winter months, I was always so cold and this little bag of heat and comfort brought me just that, comfort.

I survived the rest of the week at work, again hoping that I would wake up and magically feel better one day during the week... I did not! That weekend we had so many activities planned, my goal was to try to enjoy the action-packed weekend and then call Dr. Haynes the next Monday. Leisha was knee deep in wedding plans and we had my friend Mary coming in from out of town to assist us in reception decorating planning. She is an interior designer and volunteered to be "the woman" for the reception, we gladly and gratefully accepted that offer. We planned to go to the wedding and reception venues, take pics, measurements and notes and then the next day attend a wedding show in town.

On Sunday, the day of the wedding show, my best friend Chris volunteered to come along and finalize some wedding shower plans as well. Sunday evening, I offered to cook steaks on the grill, yes, in February! It was cloudy, windy and 42 degrees, but I willingly cooked the steaks outside. We had a wonderful time with everyone, but I was internally counting the minutes until Monday morning when I could finally call the doctor. Chris had been insistently begging me to go back to the doctor since December and she was so happy that I was finally going to do so.

Monday morning came, I tried to roll out of bed for work... it did not happen. My stomach was so distended, sore and now painful that I could not bring myself to come out from under my comfy blanket. Instead, I grabbed my cell phone and text the insurance agent that I am an account manager for, Chad, to let him know I could not be in to work and that I was calling Dr. Haynes. I hesitantly dialed the number to my doctor and they informed me they were booked for that day, they could not see me until the next day on Tuesday, February 28th.

I took the first appointment they had open, then immediately called my Mom to tell her I was staying home and seeing Dr. Haynes the following morning. Mom had persistently told me that I needed to be seen by a medical professional for several months, she would say, "Honey, you just look sickly" … bless her heart, she is typically correct and this was no exception.

Needless to say, Mom was so relieved that I had finally made an appointment that she offered to have her and Pops drive me to Dr. Hayne's office the next morning. I accepted the invitation, hung up, rolled back over on my back, covered over and fell asleep until afternoon.

I woke up from my very long and overdue nap and as I laid in bed all cozy and warm, all I could hear was the wintry wind blowing outside and I was so grateful I had stayed home.

My thoughts drifted to the past several months, how did I get here? I rested my hand on my very big belly and rubbed it gently, again, how did I let it get this far?

In my defense, I had been to see my doctor a couple of times in the past several months, I had tried to stay on top of my health, right? Then I retraced our moments during our trip to Kentucky and Tennessee a couple weeks prior, I looked through the pictures we took, I had not even shared with my family how sick I truly was.

My next thoughts went to my appointment the next morning, maybe it will be something small, insignificant, and treatable with medicine… maybe? One thing was for certain, our road trip was the last big event that would lead us into the journey that was to follow.

TWO

MY DOCTOR SAID, STAT!

I woke up Tuesday morning and drove over to my parents' house, as typical, they were ready to go before I even arrived there. I was a few minutes late because I was moving extremely slow that morning. Pops drove us to Dr. Haynes office which is only a few minutes' drive from their home.

We walked in to the office, waited the typical waiting time and then the nurse, whom I have grown to love, walked out and called my name to come back. Mom and I got up to head back to the patient exam rooms and my nurse looked at me as if she had seen a ghost, I was not sure why. Then Dr. Haynes came around the corner and gave me a similar look, she said, "You just don't look like yourself, dear, I am so glad you came in!" At that moment, I was very glad, too.

The nurse took us into the weight room, as I always call it, the room that they weigh their patients in. She had me step on the scales and I weighed 119 lbs., more than I had weighed in November, that was good, I thought. She smiled and kindly walked us back to our exam room.

Dr. Haynes, along with her sweet nurse, came in the room and they both had worried looks on their faces. Seeing them look so concerned made my heart sink into my bloated tummy. I felt like I was twelve years old again and all of the sudden, I was so grateful that my Mom had decided to come back with me to this appointment.

Dr. Haynes began to ask me the typical questions and I suppose I gave her pretty common answers for me. The big difference this time was the abnormal bloating in my abdomen. I explained all of my symptoms to her ... bloated stomach, unexplained weight loss, taking an excessive amounts of Tums, extreme fatigue, chills, no appetite and always feeling full and my periods becoming more abnormal.

She had me lay back on the table, okay, this seemed normal, but then she and my Mom saw my stomach for the first time. My doctor is probably one of the sweetest, most kind and thoughtful physicians I have ever known, her face showed both concern and confusion as to why I would have such a perfectly round belly! She even made the statement that it looked like I had a basketball in my tummy!

Dr. Haynes did not hesitate, she was very calm and direct and stated that I needed to get an abdominal, pelvic and transvaginal ultrasound, as well as blood work, STAT! She utilized that word more than I had ever heard it before or ever wanted to hear it. She scheduled the tests for later that afternoon.

We left the office and headed home for a few minutes before we had to head over to Memorial Hospital, our local hospital here in Fremont. I drove Mom and I over to the hospital and we walked in and started through the registration process. Registration was about the only thing that went normally that afternoon. The ultrasound tech came out and called me back to the ultrasound room and we made small talk on the way back.

After she had me lie down and started the ultra sound, that is when everything went from routine to anything except. Typically, when I had ultrasounds before, the tech and I would carry on a conversation, laugh, joke, etc... Not on this day! She was very sweet and kind, but she barely uttered a word as she ran the wand over my upper abdomen, over and over again. She did ask me if I had blood work done yet and I told her that was next. She finished the ultrasounds and then someone else walked in and said, "These results need to get to Dr. Haynes, (you guessed it), STAT!" That word again!

Next, we made our way to the lab to get blood work done. After some issues with receiving the orders for the blood work, they were able to get what they needed and we could finally head home. We were glad to be finished and almost out the door when a nurse came urgently down the hall way calling my name and trying to get our attention. They called us back to the same ultrasound room and the same tech, Dr. Haynes had requested an additional pelvic view. She completed the ultrasound, wished me luck and we were truly on our home this time!

I decided to spend the night at my parent's home because Pops has a recliner that I was able to rest better in and it was a much better option than trying to get in and out of my bed at home. Leisha brought a change of clothes for me and also seemed very concerned, especially when she realized that I just did not have the energy to drive home and get my own clothes!

Wednesday morning, March 1st, Dr. Haynes called me. She asked how I was doing and how I slept, she was her normal calm, comforting and kind self. Surprising to me, she already had results from the ultrasounds the day before! She explained that my ultrasound showed fluid in my abdomen and also that my ovaries were very "cysty". She went on to say that we needed to go back to the hospital that afternoon to have a CT scan with contrast of my abdomen. They also needed to drain the fluid off of my stomach for a two-fold purpose, first of all, to give me relief from the weight of the fluid; secondly, so that they could test the fluid.

After she finished her explanations, I finally said, "So, Doc, what are we looking for with the fluid?" A very short, but meaningful pause occurred and she quietly said, "Lynn, we are looking for cancer". I remember sitting there for a moment letting those last few words soak in, "Lynn, we are looking for cancer." Mom walked out and asked me what she said and I rather robotically repeated that last phrase back to her... she did not seem as surprised as I felt inside.

That afternoon, we had the CT scan with contrast done, I had to drink a large Styrofoam cup of water laced with dye. It was not easy to get all of that in an already full stomach, but I was determined and with Mom's encouragement, down it went! The ultrasound went smoothly with the same kind technician. Then they sent me upstairs to get my "basketball" drained!

A young guy came in the room, he was the technician who would be draining my tummy, he was very nice and we talked about Ohio State as I had all OSU gear on that day. He explained the procedure and it went just as he had told me, even down to the fact that Lidocaine would burn when it went in and it certainly did! After that though, I felt nothing. I merely had to lay there and watch the catheter and tube drain into a bottle beside me, not one, but TWO liters! This explains why my weight had been better at Dr. Haynes office the day before, eight pounds of the weight disappeared as they did the draining procedure!

After they finished up with the draining process, another nurse walked in the room and said the same thing they had said the day before, "Dr. Haynes needs these results... STAT!" At this point, I began to realize that the more I heard that word, the more serious the situation was becoming!

They concluded with the tests and they helped me get into a wheel chair and took me back down to the waiting room, my sister Pam was sitting with Mom. I was so relieved to see that Mom did not have to sit there all by herself through this long ordeal. Pam was very happy to see me and she and Mom asked the nurse for a snack for me while they waited to make sure I was strong enough to go home.

Apparently, I bounced back quickly from the procedure because when they did my vitals, everything seemed good and I was stable enough to go home. Pam went out and brought her van around and picked me up right at the door, the weather had turned ugly, wet and cold; after all, it was March 1st in Fremont, Ohio!

As we drove back to my parent's house, Pam and I talked about the events of the day, I filled her in on all that had occurred and what Dr. Haynes said that morning. Pam was very comforting and we even laughed about me having my "basketball" drained! In the quiet moments that followed, I could not help but hear the word "STAT", over and over in my mind… I had no idea though, how immediate, STAT really meant!

We had only been back at Mom and Pop's place a little while when Dr. Haynes office called and asked for me. The nurse said the results were back from our tests and then she asked if someone could bring me to the office at 5:15 to talk to the good doc, before we hung up, she said, "Lynn, make sure someone comes with you." Her voice sounded very serious, yet kind, I heard so much more than what had actually been said in the short conversation. I hung up, shared with Mom and Pam what was said and Pam immediately said, "Don't worry sis, I will go with you!"

We sat and talked as we waited for the time to head back to the doctor's office, as we did, all I kept thinking in my mind was "My doctor said, STAT!"

THREE

The Diagnosis

Isn't it funny how sixty minutes ticks the same on every clock and watch, but those sixty minutes can seem like one hour or five hours depending on the circumstances? On Wednesday, March 1st, our ticks seemed to slow down to a distinct and deafening crawl … Pam, Mom and I tried to rest and relax. We talked about everything … except what 5:15 p.m. might bring.

Finally, the time came for Pam and I to head out to meet with Dr. Haynes, after hours, at her office. As we drove there we talked about the weather, it had turned cloudy, windy and colder that afternoon, it seemed appropriate for the way the week had gone thus far. We got to the doctor's office and walked in to what is typically a hectic and busy place, not this day, it was extremely calm and quiet in the waiting room.

The nurse came out and explained that there was one patient remaining with the doctor so we could come back to a room and wait for her. We walked down the same hallway I had walked down so many times before, why did it seem so much longer today? She walked us down to the very last room on the left, I had never been in this particular exam room before. My sister and I walked in and sat down, the nurse made small talk with us, then left us to wait on Dr.

Haynes.

Dr. Haynes came in, I introduced her to Pam and we talked and laughed a bit as she sat down in front of us with an extremely full folder. She opened up the folder and explained that she had preliminary results from all of the tests we had been through in the past twenty-four hours. She started going over each page of the reports with us in her kind, thoughtful and caring tone. She explained that the fluid they drained from my abdomen had been sent off to be tested and that we should have the results from that back, you guessed it, STAT!

My doctor further explained the findings of the ultrasound and CT scans … I listened intently until she said, "The pelvic ultrasound showed what we believe to be tumors on both ovaries." She continued by saying that there were also nodules on my abdomen wall which looked like tumors as well. I think at that point I was looking at her and nodding and probably appeared to look engaged in the conversation, but I was not. My mind suddenly and abruptly shut down.

Pam listened for me and asked the questions that needed to be asked. After what seemed like an eternity, Dr. Haynes finally concluded the explanation of the "book" of results. She made sure to use words like "we think ", "appears to be", "it looks like", "could possibly be", etc… So, I looked at her straight in the eyes and asked the question, "Heather, what do you think it is?" She looked at me with tears in her eyes and said, "Lynn, I think you have ovarian cancer that has spread."

I tried to swallow which seemed rather difficult. Sis reached over and grabbed my had and she said something to me that has comforted me every day since, she simply said, "Sis, God is NOT surprised!" My doctor was so happy that we mentioned God and prayer, she seemed relieved that we believed in a Source and a Healer that is stronger than anything we will ever face.

The conversation turned from results to what's next… my doctor said she had a Gynecologist/Oncologist Specialist at Cleveland Clinic, Dr. Mahdi, she had made an appointment for me to see him on Friday morning if I was willing to get there. Of course, we said definitely we would be there and was so grateful that she was able to get me in so quickly! We got up to leave the room and Dr. Haynes gave us both big hugs and said she would be praying for us and wished us well. We turned and walked out the door towards our long walk back down the same hall way, although somehow nothing seemed the same.

We got to the exit doors, it was getting dark as we had been there quite some time. My phone was exploding up with concerned family and friends wanting to know how it went. I just could not even bring myself to answer any of them! Pam and I grabbed each other's hands and shared some tears as we walked out to her van.

As we got into the van I looked over at her and told her that I could not get a certain song out of my head, she looked at me very puzzled as if to say, why are you thinking about a song right now?! I started singing Tim McGraw's song, "Live Like You Were Dying." We looked at each other and started laughing… she then informed me that no matter what I was NOT going to ride a bull named Fu-man-chu!

We kept each other relatively light hearted on the drive back to our parent's home, then we pulled into the drive way. We walked in together knowing that we were going to have to face my Momma and Pops and explain the whole situation to them. We came in and sat down at the bar, Mom could tell by looking at our faces that it was what we all had feared. I relayed the information to my parent's, I tried to stay very positive as I explained a very frightening scenario.

We all broke down slightly and then I swallowed very hard, said a prayer and looked up at everyone and said, "Okay, what's for supper?" Mom had cooked a delightful meal for us, as she always does, and we all ate well. In the back of my mind I kept thinking of the rest of the evening and the dreaded chore of talking to the rest of our family.

After supper, we all walked into the living room and sat down, I was nestled back in the recliner and we all just sat in silence. The TV was on and the news was playing. I am not sure that any of us were even paying attention to a word that was said, but it was on, just the same. I started reflecting on the past twenty-four hours and all that had taken place. What a difference one day can make!

As the evening progressed Pam's daughter Cassidy came over, my daughter-in-law Ali, and my brother-in-law David (Pam's husband). My kids were both working, Leisha, at the jewelry store and my son Luke, at the factory. Leisha had been at work when I was at my appointment and she would not accept my text that said, "We will talk about it later", I had to give her a brief summary via text. Luke knew I had an appointment, but did not have access to his phone.

All of this being said, I told family one by one as they came over and everyone had a different response. Leisha arrived before Luke, she sat and talked to me and then disappeared. I finally found her and Cassidy (whom I call, Roles), in the guest room, Leisha was on the floor and having a meltdown. We found out that while Leisha was at work she Googled my diagnosis, the results were not pretty, that is why she was having a good cry. I squatted down on the floor beside her and hugged her and when she was settled down we all came back out to the living room with the rest of the family.

After we all sat down out there, we all pinky-swore that we would not Google anything else, period. All of the sudden Roles spoke up and said, "Google is NOT God!" We all whole-heartedly agreed and we have tried to stick to that very important pinky-swear!

I finally made myself get out of the recliner and headed into the kitchen for a drink, there at the bar sat David, he looked very concerned and sad. I sat down beside him, as I looked up at him I thought about all of the years of my life that David had been there for me. David had been my Youth Pastor, basketball coach, teacher and mainly my friend. The fact that later in life he became my brother-in-law was merely icing on the cake for me... I always knew I could count on him for advice, no matter what the situation. After a few minutes of silence, I said, "So, David, what do you think?" He looked back at me, wiped a few tears away and said, "I think you've got this and you have all of us beside you, whatever you need, I will be here for you!" I gave him a big hug and for a moment in time, I felt like a high school kid all over again, looking to her "coach" for encouragement and hope and I found both in David as I had so many times before.

Finally, Luke was off work, Ali text him and asked him to stop at my parent's house. From that point on, Luke knew something was up, the fact that he was summonsed to my parent's (referred to fondly by the family as Nana and Papa's) at 11:00 p.m. meant something big. Luke came in and by-passed everyone sitting in the living room, which is not like him, and came directly over to me. He kneeled down on the floor beside my recliner and said, "What's up Momma?" I told him exactly what the doctor said, I had to say the words again, they think I have ovarian cancer that has spread!

Luke had tears in his eyes, but he quickly wiped those away and looked at me and said, "We've got this, Momma!" Everyone in the room had the same look, a look of strength and hope.

That night as I closed my eyes and tried so hard to fall asleep all I could think about was my diagnosis ... that and a bull named Fu-Man-Chu!

FOUR

WILL I LAST LONGER THAN MY TOOTHPASTE?

I have to be honest, the day after my preliminary diagnosis I truly did nothing except lay in my recliner. I did not want to eat, I did not respond to friends and family on my phone, and I literally just laid there. For the first time in my life my mind was blank, I was not over-thinking anything, I was not thinking at all! I think that I was numb, period. The only thing that broke up the day was Dr. Hayne's call later in the afternoon to confirm that the tests on the fluid they drained definitely showed the origin as bilateral Ovarian Cancer.

I knew the next day I had to head to Cleveland Clinic to the Cancer Center, wait, I HAVE TO GO TO THE CANCER CENTER! We truly never know what tomorrow brings, do we?

David had volunteered to chauffeur me and my entourage to Cleveland and I so happily accepted his offer. It was so bitterly cold outside and David's new van had heated seats!! Leisha, Pam and Role's offered to go with us to meet our Gynecologist/Oncologist, Dr. Haider Mahdi.

We left that icy morning for Cleveland, we packed snacks, bundled up and headed out. David had my seat all toasty warm for me and it felt extremely wonderful. David had good music on his XM radio and our only rule was that we would not listen to any sad songs whatsoever and we did not! About half way there I blurted out, "Hey, most people who have cancer get a t-shirt, I want a t-shirt!" I heard laughing from the back seat as they pondered my not so deep thought of the moment... I just wanted a t-shirt!

As we were discussing t-shirt options, the kids were in the back of the van busily looking up Ovarian Cancer, finally one of the girls mentioned that teal was the color that represented this disease. I thought about it for a minute and then decided that I did not want teal, "I dislike Ovarian Cancer very much and I do not want anything to do with the color that represents it!" Of course, everyone in the van understood my reasoning... that is not always easy, let me tell you! I determined that I wanted purple, purple is cheery, or that was my first thought! Roles spoke up again and reminded us that purple always represents the Lord and His majesty in the Bible; that confirmed it for us, purple it was!

As we got closer to Cleveland the traffic picked up and the reality began to set in again, we are going to an appointment with an Oncologist this morning, not just any Oncologist... Dr. Mahdi, a specialist in his field! I said a prayer, not a little one, a big one, took a deep breath and tried to prepare my mind for what was going to take place in a matter of minutes.

Cleveland Clinic is enormous, it is like a city in itself, as we weaved our way through the streets that were affiliated with the Clinic I was in awe at the vastness of this hospital! David so graciously dropped us off at the front doors, Roles, Sis, Leish and I got out and arm in arm, we walked in together, a united front! We walked into a monstrosity of a lobby and went to the information desk. The lady was so friendly and she kindly gave us the lay of the land and let us know where my doctor's office was located in the building.

I mentioned earlier that my cousin Jayne is a nurse, at that time, she worked at Cleveland Clinic and other hospitals in the area. That particular day, she made sure she was at the Clinic, so I text her to let her know we had arrived. We waited for David and then we all made our way up to Dr. Mahdi's office.

I cannot explain what a wonderfully calming sight it was to walk into the huge office waiting room and see Jayne! She came straight over to us and gave me a huge hug and introduced me to the ladies at the front desk. I had paperwork and registration to complete at a computer so Leisha came over and helped me accomplish all of that. I had just finished the paperwork when a nurse came out and called my name. Sis had offered to come back with me to my appointment and I was so glad she did!

We went back to the examination room and the nurse, Jennifer, asked me questions and prepared me for my meeting with the doctor. The nurse walked out and Pam and I talked while we were checking out this exam room, it was very different than any room I had ever been in before. There were plastic models of female organs and large posters explaining different types of cancer. We did not have to wait very long though and in walked Dr. Mahdi.

He was not what I had imagined, he looked very young, handsome and had the kindest face. He came over and introduced himself to us, shook our hands and then plopped down on the stool and slid over to sit closer to us. He moved straight over to the computer screen and pulled up my test results which he was very familiar with, he obviously had reviewed them prior to our appointment. He pointed out different nodules and masses.

Dr. Mahdi wrote a number on the piece of paper in front of him and I squinted to see the number he wrote down. He reached over and held my hand and said, "My dear, this is just a number, nothing to worry about!" He picked up the paper and showed me that it said, "Stage 3", at that very moment, I had my first official break down. Sis and I definitely had a moment at the same time, I guess the reality of the stage sunk in rather quickly.

Dr. Mahdi kept patting my hand and he said, "You are too young, I will take great care of you, you are too young for this, you will be fine, my dear!" He then went on to explain that he would need to do extensive surgery, he would do a full hysterectomy and remove any visible cancer. He saw a tumor in the lower bowel and he expected to have to remove part of my bowel, thus, he fully expected for me to come out of surgery with a colostomy bag. He then explained that they found a small amount of fluid in my left lung and that we had to re-scan that to ensure that was not indicative of cancer. If cancer was in my lung it would move me to Stage 4 and I would need to have chemo for 4-5 weeks, then attempt surgery. So, he would schedule another CT scan with contrast to determine this as soon as possible.

After he explained the surgery he went on to post surgery, I would have approximately 5-6 weeks to recover and then begin a strong regimen of chemotherapy, every week for 18 weeks!

The doctor left the room for a bit and Sis and I were able to sit and soak in all that was said, goodness, there was so much information to digest! While Dr. Mahdi was out of the room I decided it was time to pull myself together, so I wiped the tears away and again, took one of those deep cleansing breaths! I looked up at my sister and said, "In it to win it!" She said, "What, sis??" I repeated the same thing again, "In it to win it! That's what I want to put on my t-shirts, that is our motto!" She smiled at me and agreed.

Dr. Mahdi came back in, I told him what my motto was going to be, he smiled and gave an approving nod. He had been able to schedule my surgery for Tuesday, March 14th. When he said the date, I looked sad, he said, "You look upset, is that a bad date?" I explained that my daughter was getting married in May and her bridal shower was going to be on March 18th. The kind doctor said, "I did not know you had a 'to-do', I can fit you in on March 25th if that would work better for you?" I already adored this man and I had only known him for one hour.

He told me to think about the surgery date while he performed a pelvic exam, he did that and his nurse (who was actually a doctor in training) performed one as well. It was very uncomfortable during the procedures and he apologized several times to me because he could tell that it was. He let me know that he was able to actually feel the mass as he did the exam, I knew that could not be a good thing.

After the exams, he allowed Pam and I to go out and up-date everyone and decide on the surgery date. We went out to the lobby and called everyone over, Jayne, Roles and Leisha joined us in a huddle in the waiting room. We explained everything and I looked at Jayne and asked her my burning question, "Should I wait until after the shower or should I do it on the 14th?" Jayne did not hesitate before she told me to ask Dr. Mahdi what his preference was and go with that! We all came close together and Jayne led us in prayer, a prayer for guidance, strength, healing and unity. Jennifer came out at the end of our prayer and joined our little huddle for a moment and then said we needed to come back and finish up with Dr. Mahdi.

Again, Sis and I walked back through the hallway to the exam room and there sat Dr. Mahdi, I sat down beside him and asked him to tell me his preference on the surgery. He calmly and quietly said, "I would rather get it done on the 14th, I'm sorry about your 'to-do" my dear, but that is my preference." I grabbed his hand and said, I trust you, let's get this done!

We walked out of the office into the waiting room, David was pacing on the other side of the room. He looked up and saw us and called me over, he hugged me and said, "Lynn, whatever you need, I am here, anytime you need to come to Cleveland, I will be your driver, anything else you need, we will take care of you!" Again, he was such a comfort at a time I needed it most.

Once again, the girls and I walked arm in arm down to the lobby to wait on David to bring the van back up to the doors. We piled into the van and started on the drive home. The first thing I informed them was that our motto for our t-shirt and for our journey was set, "In it to win it!" To my surprise, they all thought it was perfect! Next on our agenda was how to inform the family and others about the results of my meeting with Dr. Mahdi!

Leisha drafted a text to send out to family and close friends and we made a few calls to my Mom, Eric and the next call had to be to my work family. This is a good place to tell you a little bit about my job.

I am an Account Manager for both small and large groups who have their benefits and insurance with UIS Insurance and Investments, my second home and place of employment. I work in the Fremont office with the BEST co-workers ever, they are, indeed, my second family. There is Deb, Collette, Linda, Nancy, Lois, Paul and my best friend, Chris. I mostly work with Chad, who is the main agent in our office, he is more like a brother to me than a boss.
Chad and I just clicked from the very beginning… we have so much in common, especially our love and knowledge of the Ohio State Buckeyes football team! He quizzes me often on my knowledge of new recruits for the Buckeyes, injury up-dates, etc… Chad, along with the others, make work fun.

With all of that being said, the next call had to be to them. So, I called Chris's cell phone, she placed me on speaker phone and I told all of them the entire situation. I even told them about my motto, they were on board with the #inittowinit theme. They let me know that they would be there for me no matter what and in Collette's words, "You've got this, Lynn!"

We made the journey home and it was such a relief to have this out of the way and all the details squared away. I could already tell that I had the most amazing support team ever, between my family and close friends, God had blessed me with the best and I felt so much gratitude.

While I was gone, Mom had decided that I was moving in with them, as in, today! So, they had already brought some of my necessities over from my apartment. As I walked back to the guest room which was now going to be my room, I saw the various items sitting on the bed. Amidst the "stuff" there was a huge stack of toothpaste. My future son-in-law and my parents had purchased a large supply of my Crest Citrus Splash for me. I am allergic to mint, right, who is allergic to mint?? Thus, I can use a very limited variety of tooth paste! This particular one was discontinued so they stocked up for me, literally, 10 tubes of my toothpaste sat there! As I looked at it, the first thought that came to my head was "Will I out last my toothpaste supply?" I felt the tears welling up and then I re-thought what just went through my mind and it actually made me chuckle!

What a big day this had been! I was introduced to the most amazing surgeon ever and at the end of the day, will I outlast my toothpaste??? It was such a good thing that I could learn to laugh at the silly details, laughing truly can be one of the BEST medicines!

FIVE

ANOTHER ROAD TRIP

After our big road trip to Cleveland, I found myself in a zone again, not necessarily a good one, either. I noticed fluid beginning to build up again, this time in my lower back, it had not been there before. I spoke with my cousin Jayne about it and she let me know that I had to start getting up and moving, I needed to start eating and drinking more and I had to get my determination back if I was ever going to be strong enough for surgery! My immediate family had been trying to tell me the same things … finally, I listened!

I determined right then and there that I would start eating three meals a day, getting out of the recliner to do things such as: take a shower and begin gaining mental stamina! My Mom was shocked the most by these changes because I had not eaten well in so long. I started eating a good breakfast, hardy lunch and even an adequate supper, something I had not been able to do in such a long time. My positive changes, in addition to hours of prayer, revitalized my whole being.

I began responding to text messages, phone calls, Facebook messages, and even allowed David to start a Prayer Warrior page for me via Facebook. The interaction with people really started inspiring me in ways I did not think were possible at the time. My immediate family were constantly encouraging me, calling me, and cheering me on. We started allowing dear friends to stop in for visits, some folks I had not seen in years and years. The visits were such a blessing and really helped motivate me to keep going.

My repeat CT scan to re-inspect the fluid in my lung was set for Wednesday, March 8th, bright and early in the morning at the Sandusky Offices of Cleveland Clinic. They scheduled it then, so that we could have the results back before I was scheduled to go to my Pre-Op appointment at main campus on that Friday. The afternoon before my scan we had the most bizarre winds I have ever seen in this part of Ohio, it was warm, but winds in excess of 60 mph! The morning of my scan a receptionist called to inform me that my particular CT machine had been damaged by those winds and that they could not repair it! What are the odds?

Cleveland Clinic, main campus, was able to re-schedule my CT to take place there on Friday morning (extremely early) before my Pre-Op schedule started. So, that was the new plan! David so graciously offered to take Leisha and I on yet another road trip to Cleveland on Friday, March 10th, for my scan and the long morning of Pre-Op appointments. We had to leave at 5:00 a.m. and believe it or not, all of us were alert on the way there! David had my favorite heated seats turned on for me and I was grateful and warm all the way to Cleveland.

We arrived at the Cancer Center once again and surprisingly it did not seem as big to me as it had just one week before. We walked down to the CT scan area, it was a very sterile looking hallway in the middle of nowhere in a basement. David and Leisha had to wait in the waiting area for me while I went back for the actual test. It was a very sophisticated and smooth system they had, I went straight back to a triage area to have my IV inserted for the dye which would come during the procedure. Immediately following that I was escorted to a holding room for everyone waiting on scans, I walked in the room and it was evident that every person in there had cancer. Some had very little hair, some looked very ill and others looked fatigued and fearful. As I sat there, I started praying for the patients I was sitting with, I remember thinking to myself that these people were extremely sick. Then for one of the first times a lightbulb went off in my head, hey, I am extremely sick, too!

The technician came to the door and called my name, I had to tell them my date of birth and what stage my cancer was, this was such a reality moment for me. We went back and completed the scan and he let me know that I would find out the results of this very important scan by 5:00 p.m.. Finally, I was able to reunite with my daughter and David who were very patiently waiting.

We headed back over to the Cancer Center and began the rigorous schedule of pre-operation appointments. I had to do things like an EKG, more blood work, and even see a hospital physician for a physical examination. The doctor who saw me that day remarked about how healthy I appeared with my blood work and medical history, the only abnormality in my blood work was that I was anemic. The doctor was very kind, wished me well and sent us to my last station.

We had to go talk to a counselor about a clinical trial they were doing with Ovarian cases like mine which required surgery. They wanted me to sign two different consents, #1 is permission to give me blood if I needed it during or after surgery. #2 is to take an epidural instead of pain medication following my surgery. I signed consent for #1, but I declined on #2 because I did not know enough about it.

As David, Leisha and I were walking out we ran into Jayne again, she was such a breath of fresh air and reminded me that I was in the best place in the world for what I was going through. In my heart, I totally believed that was the case and I was once again grateful!

We drove home and Leisha and I sat and waited on the crucial phone call from Dr. Mahdi's nurse which would tell us the results of the scan and if I could go through with the surgery or have to take chemo treatments first. After what seemed like hours, my cell phone rang, of course we were both out of the room and missed the call! Noooooo!

I looked at my most recent call and sure enough, it was Cleveland Clinic's number! I hit the voicemail and put my cell on speaker so Leisha and I could hear it together! Jennifer's voice sounded very positive as she relayed that Dr. Mahdi had looked at the scan and agreed that I was good to go for surgery! I actually teared up with joy as that is what we had been praying for all along.

Leisha and I rejoiced in the good news and then reality hit us again… Tuesday I would be going in for the biggest surgery of my life! Now is the time to cling to our hashtags and not just write them in a text … #inittowinit #Godsnotsurprised #allin4Lynn

Now that we had an official date of my surgery, we started the process of letting family members and close friends know the details, as well as up-dating our Prayer Warrior page on Facebook. A little bit later that night my brother called me to let me know that they had up-dated Colton on my condition and that surgery was happening in a few days. Later that evening Colton walked in where Eric and Mer were sitting and said, "I have the perfect verse for Aunt Lynnie, Philippians 4:13, I can do all things through Christ who strengthens me!"

I was so completely touched by the sincere and loving thoughts of an almost 9-year-old boy, tears filled my eyes and fell down my cheeks. What a precious boy and a perfect verse for me. Colton had no idea how much his verse would help get me through some of the darkest and toughest times of my life that were yet to come!

#IcandoallthingsthroughChrist

SIX

YOU MUST TRUST ME!

The days that led up to my surgery resulted in so many visitors, even some that I had not seen in years! The visits were very encouraging to me, so many people cared, I had no idea!

 I did notice that some people would visit out of guilt for something they had carried with them for a very long time that happened between us, things I did not even remember! These friends came to ask forgiveness or to make amends and I assured those folks that I did not even remember the offense and no apologies were needed. Somethings in life are just not that important at the end of the day…

So many dear friends would come through the door, see me and then burst into tears, I understand, I have been on the other side of cancer. One thing was true with each visit, it always ended happily, reassuringly and with a promise to pray for me throughout this journey!

I woke up on Monday, March 13th with the knowledge that this is finally THE DAY BEFORE! I had a few friends dropping by and then I had to begin the "bowel clean out" process. This "fun" activity included taking 4 antibiotics within 2 hours of each other, as well as drinking a liquid posing as something with a grape flavoring, in all reality, it tasted like grape salt! Between the mixture of all of this, I ended up getting extremely nauseated and throwing up.

My nurse called to check on me and I told her I had gotten sick, she informed me that I did not have to finish the antibiotic that made me so nauseated. I was relieved! After I hung up from my nurse, I looked outside and there it was, the fluffy, magical white stuff I have always loved! SNOW!!! I laid back in my recliner, watched the snow fall outside and thanked God for sending me this sign of comfort.

As the day progressed, the magical goodness of the snow turned into a concern that we had to travel to Cleveland very early the next morning! We were afraid to leave the night before and stay in a hotel because of the bowel clean out taking effect, if it did, a long drive would not be very conducive to that scenario!

We had visitors until late that evening … finally Eric, Mer and Colton arrived. I was so happy to see them! Colton brought me his "Spidey Bear" that he had made at Build-A-Bear, he said, "Aunt Lynnie, this is the softest bear I have and I want YOU to have it, it will make you feel better! And I do not want him back, he is for you to keep!" What a precious keep sake for me to take to Cleveland Clinic and keep by my bedside!

We all sat around and talked about all kinds of things, sharing stories, laughing, and almost forgetting what the next day would bring! I did not want to fall asleep that night, so my brother and I stayed up and talked until the wee hours of the morning. (that is nothing new for us!)

My alarm went off at 4:45 a.m.…. I am not a morning person anyway, but this time, I certainly wished that I could hit snooze and stay in my recliner! I finally drug myself out of the chair and did my devotions, always one of my favorite parts of the day! I opened up my Bible to Philippians 4:13, Colton's verse for me, I read it out loud to myself,

"I can do ALL things through Christ who strengthens me."

Everyone arrived at our house for the extremely early departure, did I mention how early it was?? My niece, Crystal drove Pam's van and Mer drove her truck, I chose to ride in the truck, we knew that if anyone got stuck and could not continue the treacherous drive it would NOT be her F150!

We headed out to Cleveland in a significant snow storm, the weather had predicted up to one foot of snow at our destination. The drive was uneventful except for the fact that my bowel clean out delayed it's affect until on my way to the Clinic, really??? I felt so horrible that we had to stop for me to go to the restroom, but everyone was so kind and patient with me.

We arrived at the Clinic at about 7:30 a.m., Mer dropped Leisha, Colton and I off at the door and we entered an enormous lobby area. As we walked through, Colton spotted a wishing fountain, it was so beautiful, of course we all had to put some coins in it and even though we did not say it out loud, I believe each one of us had the same wish!

We met everyone upstairs and the hospital was ready for me! Leisha was given a pager to hold for the day to receive up-dates on me. My surgery was supposed to start at 11:00 that morning. The kind receptionist at the desk told me it was time to leave my family and go to the holding area, my family would be permitted to come back with me after I got in my gown and the IV was in place.

I remember walking down the winding hallway with nothing but butterflies in my stomach … literally, as the clean out had definitely CLEANED me out! I came around one of the corners and I ran into Jayne, I was so relieved! She hugged me and then walked me back to admitting, she was such a comfort! I was given a gown and then a room, they inserted the IV and then called for my family to come back and sit with me for the next couple of hours until surgery.

Seeing my family walk through the halls was so entertaining. All ten people had their purple #inittowinit shirts on. The family were pretty popular at the Clinic due to those t-shirts.

Dr. Mahdi had a surgery prior to mine and it went extremely long, in fact, when I was supposed to be going up to surgery he was still in the OR with the patient before me! Hour after hour we sat and waited in a very small holding room. I remember how long the day seemed to drag on, our clocks went to a slow crawl again! My family was so amazing though, they stayed right with me even though some of them had to stand the entire time. I had Leisha, Mom, Pops, Crystal, Eric, Mer, Colty and Pam with me to help pass the hours.

At about 2:00 I asked everyone if we could join hands and say a prayer, I said, "Listen, I do not want a big prayer right before I am wheeled out of here because I will cry, so let's do it now!" I decided to lead in prayer and Colton followed me, out of the mouths of babes, he prayed the sweetest prayer ever! We all had a sentimental moment and then got back to taking selfies and making each other laugh, we even sang some songs together being silly.

After what seemed like three days, the time came for me to go up to the Operating Room area, this was the time I dreaded … I had to say, "see you later" to each one of my family members. Everyone walked by me, hugged me, kissed me and I was no longer strong, I had tears flowing down my face the entire time! A young man came to walk me up and he held my hand and kept telling me that I had always been there for others, now it is my time to take care of me. He kept saying how Dr. Mahdi would take wonderful care of me and I would be fine. He was so thoughtful and caring and I just kept crying!

We got upstairs and he had to leave me and my gurney in the hallway where I waited for the O.R. nurse to come and talk to me. Shortly, there she was, leaning over me and talking to me in a very soothing voice. After she was done ensuring they knew my allergies to medicines, etc… she wheeled me in to the O.R. WOW, it was a HUGE room and extremely bright and white!

Soon, there were four or five people around me. My nurse, a few assistants and the anesthesiologist. He explained that he would not let me become even nauseated and that he would do everything he could to keep me comfortable, again, such a compassionate and kind man. Then entered Dr. Mahdi!

He came over to me, held my hand and looked at my eyes, there were still tears welling up and some even escaping down my cheeks. He explained the surgery to me again and confirmed that depending on what he found he might have to just sew me back up and go through some chemotherapy first.

Finally, we were finished with the surgery explanation and he looked very deeply in my eyes and he said something I will never forget, "You MUST trust me!" I reassured him that I did and he held both of my hands and said, "I can tell by your eyes that you do not trust me, until I see that you do, I cannot begin the operation! You MUST trust me, first!" I knew it was Dr. Mahdi's words, but in my mind and heart I felt like God was saying the same thing to me, I had to trust!

Slowly and with difficulty, I took a deep breath, wiped away my tears and looked up at my surgeon and said, "Dr. Mahdi, I trust you and God's got this, let's do it!"

The anesthesiologist brought the big black mask over and told me to breathe in five deep breaths and count them, I felt the burn of the medicine coming into my IV and I began taking the deep breaths. I remember as I was breathing saying the verse again in my mind, "I can do ALL things through Christ who strengthens me!"

At that moment, everything went dark…. The journey had truly begun!

SEVEN

THE TAJ MAHAL

It still amazes me how quickly five hours can go when I am asleep, meaning sound asleep from anesthetic! It seemed like only moments had passed and there I was, awake and in a very quiet and sterile room. I remember looking around and seeing two nurses in front of me, to the left of me was another gurney with another post-surgical patient. She seemed very miserable and was complaining and asking questions in a very loud tone.

Okay, back to me now, I was awake, but I just laid there. None of my family was there, it was just me, was this a good sign or bad sign? I remember being so very cold, I was shivering and chattering so loudly and I could not control it. My throat was extremely sore, I remember trying to clear it and thinking I probably could not speak because it was too painful. The nurse saw my eyes open and came over to my bedside, she squeezed my hand and asked how I was doing. I told her that I was okay, then I thought, awesome, I know my voice works!

In a few minutes, I saw figures of people walking in through my peripheral vision, I felt like I could not turn my head, so I had to wait until they stood in front of me! It was Leisha and Eric, still representing in their purple #inittowinit t-shirts! I was so happy in my heart to see them! Leisha could tell I was freezing so she politely asked the nurse for blankets. The nurse brought over heated blankets and then even wrapped one around my head so that I could relax and not be so tense from being cold.

I wanted them to know that I was coherent and knew they were there, but I did not want to talk, so I merely looked at Leisha and winked. She said, "There she is, I knew my Momma would be awake!" Eric smiled at me and said how happy he was that I was okay. I remember staring at their faces trying to see if I was truly "okay" or not by their expressions. I could not read them. Finally, I asked Leisha, in my very weak voice, "What did they do in surgery?" All she kept saying was how well it went and that Dr. Mahdi was so thrilled that everything went great. My brother kept giving me similar responses.

Eric left to let someone else come back in and I whispered to Leisha, "You are my kid, tell me what they really did to me!" She gave me a brief summary which now I do not even recall and I was satisfied with her answer. More family was allowed to come back, but it was very late at night by this time, after midnight… what a LONG day for my family.

The nurses started whispering to each other, but I could hear them, they were discussing my hemoglobin count and the fact that if it did not come back up that I would need a transfusion. I remembered signing a consent form for that previously so I was covered if it was necessary. Eventually, they decided it was and they hooked up a unit of blood by my bed and it started going in. I remember watching it drip and feeling like it took an extremely L-O-N-G time for it to go in, but, alas, it was finished and I could finally head up to my room!

Some very nice orderlies came to push me the long journey up to my new residence for the next several days, "We are taking her to the G wing", I heard them say. We finally arrived to my room, 71, I could hear my family in the room waiting for me. When they wheeled me in, there was Leisha, Crystal and Pam all sitting there half asleep and very exhausted, after all, it was now 3:00 in the morning!

The nurses came and got me all hooked up to many things, made sure my vitals were okay and then left me to "rest." I looked around the room and immediately thought, am I in the Taj Mahal?? It was an enormous room, with one whole wall of windows overlooking Cleveland, it was beautiful! I assured my family that I was as comfortable as possible and one by one everyone finally fell asleep.

We woke up to the hustle and bustle of Dr. Mahdi's student assistant coming in to check on me, this became routine every day, my 6:00 a.m. wakeup call! She came in, checked out my incision, told me how good it looked and then mentioned checking on my drain tubes. Drain tubes? I had not noticed or known about drain tubes. I had two drain bulbs from my incision, one on the right and one on the bottom left. Then I looked up at the doctor and said, "Did I come out of surgery with a bag?" She smiled and assured me that I did not need a colostomy bag and what a tremendous help that would be to me.

I did not understand why my throat was so scratchy and sore, finally she explained that I had an NG tube, it was aiding in keeping my stomach from getting upset. Wow, there was so much that I did not understand or mentally prepare for, including hearing the outcome of my surgery!

My family woke up and were so eager to talk to me. I was very groggy and yet felt wide awake all at the same time. I asked them again, "What happened in my surgery?" Crystal, Pam and Leisha began explaining the surgery to me... "Well, Dr. Mahdi was very pleased with how everything went and you do not have a colostomy bag!" Then they continued to explain that he found much more cancer than what he had previously expected.

I had cancer in both ovaries, thus the full hysterectomy, additionally, it was in my lower bowel (which he was able to take the tumor then reattach my bowel), diaphragm, upper abdominal wall, pelvic wall, pancreas, bladder and right kidney. Dr. Mahdi removed my spleen and appendix because they had cancer in them as well. WHOA, what just happened?? I just laid there and took it all in, or tried to. How could it be possible that I was that full of cancer? But, Dr. Mahdi got all of the visible cancer, so that was good, right?

I was in so much pain, the nurse came in and introduced us to the pain pump, it contained Dilaudid. The nurse explained that I could hit the pump every 10 minutes if needed, I decided against that immediately. I watched the clock and would hit the pump once an hour, no more than that! I was afraid the medicine would make me sick and I just did not want to be totally out of it, I am much too nosey for that!

The rest of my family arrived and to everyone's surprise my room was large enough to handle as many of us as we wanted to fit in there! It was truly the nicest hospital room I had ever seen! I was so relieved to see everyone and know that the surgery was truly over with! I was a big fan of having as many people in the room with me as possible, I even suggested they eat in and take phone calls in my room!

As the nurses shuffled in and out, I learned right away what they were looking for. They checked my drainage tubes and would have to flush them which was not my favorite because it stung. They checked vitals, as well as my Foley Catheter to keep close eye on my urine output.

Later on, the first day they decided to try to have me sit up and get into a chair, I cringed at the thought. They came in and sat the head of my bed in an upright position… immediately the room started spinning. Then they attempted to have me sit on the side of my bed, the room spun worse and I felt like I was going to pass out. They had me lay back down and gave me anti-nausea medicine in my IV. I was basically in and out all day and that night.

My family had a schedule all figured out so that I was never in the room by myself, not even for bed time, they stayed around the clock! Some of my family stayed in a hotel right by the hospital, that made it convenient for them as they were trying to stay all week. My mom was always there, trying to talk to me, comfort me, and calm me. I was not very pleasant nor engaging, I do not really remember it very well, but I still feel badly that I did not appear to be very gracious during those first few days!

I still remember the first time I was actually able to get up and sit in a chair, when they took out my Foley, took me off of the pain pump, etc... Each tiny victory and each baby step led to another and another. Each nurse I encountered was so kind and encouraging. My favorite part of the day was when Dr. Mahdi would come in, typically early in the morning. He would check on me, discuss the same questions I asked over and over again and was never anything except happy and positive, "You are doing GREAT, my dear, I am so proud of you!", is what he would say on a daily basis.

Finally, my mom was helping me get to the restroom one day and I wanted to look at my incision, I had avoided that until this moment. She assisted me in moving my layers of gowns so that I could see it. Thirty-four staples!!! It was the craziest, yet cleanest incision I had ever seen. I was cut from below my breasts all the way down. I felt relieved after I saw it though, yet, another hurdle we were able to get me over!

As the week progressed I was finally allowed to try a liquid diet. I remember the first time I took a sip of broth how it seemed to burn all the way down until it hit my stomach. I saw progress each time I ate though, I was able to eat a tiny bit more each attempt. It's amazing how we take certain everyday things for granted, like being able to eat. I was never so thankful to see Cream of Wheat, that was the first thing that tasted good, next it was oatmeal with brown sugar and so on…

I have always adored my family and felt like I appreciated them, but never as much as that week. I have the most amazing family members, each hospital staff member we encountered commented on the uncommon closeness that my family represented that week.

I explained that my family is consistently that way, not just during a hospital stay. I was so very grateful that I did not have to endure the very LONG nights there by myself. The nurses were amazing, but nothing takes the place of a family member sliding their very uncomfortable reclining chair right beside my bed and having a "sleep over" with me.

There was one special nurse, his name was Beau. I thoroughly enjoyed the over nights with him because he was so kind and nurturing, but also because he told me very interesting historical facts about our wing of the Cleveland Clinic. For instance, Beau told me about the time that the Shah of Iran had prostate cancer, back in the 1970's. He rented out the entire G-wing for him and his staff members to come to the Clinic. He stayed in my room! Beau joked that night that I was safe from snipers because the Shah actually paid to have the windows bullet proofed in my room!

Day after day went by and I started to feel a little bit stronger, I was no longer on any type of pain medication. I went from Dilaudid to Regular Strength Tylenol every six hours, my preference. My bowels were moving satisfactorily with the assistance of Colace, stool softener. I remember the day that they removed my first drain bulb, wow, that was not a fun experience whatsoever! They literally tell you to take a deep breath in and let it out slowly as they pull out the snake like tube! I always took an efficient deep breath in but letting it out slowly did not work so well for me! Either way, I was so thankful to get at least one tube out.

Dr. Mahdi came in early that Saturday morning, March 18th and informed me that I would most likely get to go home on Monday or Tuesday. I was very relieved to hear that everything was going well, but today was Leisha's bridal shower! Everyone had to head home the night before to prepare for Leisha's big day! I would be remiss if I did not mention that I was extremely depressed that I would not be in attendance or sharing in one of my kid's most memorable days before her wedding!

David was the lucky one who got to endure the wedding shower day with me, as I mentioned, I was extremely down to say the least. Around noon Jayne walked in the room, she had decorations, including gorgeous balloons to adorn my room with to make me feel like I was actually at Leisha's shower! It was the sweetest gesture and my room truly was a vision after her and David finished decorating!

I had several little break-downs that day, but everyone kept me going and focused on healing and getting stronger even on the rough days. When it was time for the Shower festivities to begin, it was a joint effort getting me access via Skype, it was absolutely amazing. Mer took her iPad around to many of the guests at the shower and we were able to chat. I was able to view the entire event including getting a front row "seat" to watch Leisha open up her gifts. I was so sad not being there, but so happy to be able to share in the day from a distance. #blessed

As the day ended and night time was upon us once again, I was so thankful for the extraordinary people God has placed in my life through family and friendships. I thought back at the day and the shower, my best friend Chris handled the entire shower for me with the assistance of my immediate family and Leisha's bridal party... what special people we are sharing this life with!

After that day, I was set on going home, that day was swiftly approaching! I had mixed emotions about leaving the confines of the Taj Mahal, but, everyone knows that there is truly no place like home!

EIGHT

THERE'S NO PLACE LIKE HOME

My final full day and night in the hospital had arrived, Nate, my nephew, was still with me and we had enjoyed so much time together. He promised to stay with me until back-ups arrived. Leisha was supposed to come that evening after work and spend the night with me and help me get ready the next day to go home. Nate stayed until my cousin Tricia, her husband Bob and their daughter Alyssa came up to visit. Their visit was such a refreshing one and I am sure Nate was ready to go home after a day and a half with the patient! (although he did not complain and stayed by my side the entire time)

Leisha text to let me know she was in the hospital, I was so excited to see her, it had been a few days. When she arrived to my room she said she had a surprise with her… she did, Luke came with her! It was amazing to spend the last night there with both of my kids, we watched tv, laughed a lot and the time together was priceless.

From the time Dr. Mahdi started discussing my departure day, I was so happy, yet had some reservations as well. Why reservations? I suppose the main reasons were that I had grown accustomed to a twenty-four hour medical staff keeping track of every little detail and I felt secure with that. Granted, I knew I was going to be recovering at the best place ever, my parent's home; yet, none of us are doctors or nurses. Would we know what to do if something went wrong? Questions like these were soon answered by my discharge nurse and Dr. Mahdi on discharge day.

Tuesday, March 21st my day started extremely early! At 6:00 a.m. Dr. Mahdi's student doctor and a nurse came in to inform me that they would be removing my last drain tube! This was both exciting and scary news, I remembered how much the first one hurt! I knew the drill, I took my deep breath in and they started tugging on the drain tube, several seconds and pains later, the tube was out!

They did a quick exam on me and let me know that everything looked good for a "ticket to ride" home today. I knew that the morning would also hold a set of immunizations for me, Dr. Mahdi had let me know that I would need a Meningococcal B Vaccine, Pneumococcal Vaccine and the HIB Vaccine because of my spleen removal, the spleen aids in fighting off infections.

Dr. Mahdi stopped in, as always, he was beaming with pride and joy that I was able to go home as scheduled. He expressed deep concern about my weight, I was 111 lbs. when I came into the hospital, the day I was released I was down to 94 lbs.! He gently warned me that if I lost the average twenty pounds that his patients typically lost I would no longer be here, so, my main goal was to EAT! Dr. Mahdi also explained, in his kind and positive way, that I would be seeing him in ten days to remove my staples and do a quick check up. Knowing I would get to see him in only ten days made me feel so much better. We posed in a pic together, then he gave me a big squeeze and said his famous line again, "I am so proud of you, my dear, you have done a wonderful job, you are going to be fine!"

The morning went by quickly, my kids did a great job in organizing my weeks' worth of belongings and getting me pumped up for the long ride home! David was on his way in my favorite van, but the heated seats were not necessary as it had warmed up to a balmy 65 degrees!

My discharge nurse finally came in with my immunizations, she warned me that three shots would not feel very good today since I had literally no spare fat to insert the needles into. Oh well, with all the last few weeks had brought my way, what would a few shots hurt? She administered the injections without too much pain, although I could tell my left arm was going to feel the effects later and it did! She also explained that I would go home needing a daily Lovenox shot, a blood thinner, that I was required to have for twenty-one more days.

As the kids helped me get dressed in REAL clothes for the first time in eight days, I was finally feeling ready to head west. In the meantime, my sweet Momma called to inform me that my best friend from high school, Sara, had offered to come to our house every day and administer my shot! I was so relieved, Sara is a nurse and someone that I trust wholeheartedly. Again, God was so good in answering each little and not so little request.

David arrived and the discharge process seemed to take forever. After stacks of paperwork had been completed and explained, it was finally time to GO HOME! I must say, Cleveland Clinic's nursing staff and doctors were absolutely phenomenal in every way, they were like extended family for that week and I was leaving there extremely grateful for their care.

David went out to get the van while the kids walked with all of my "stuff" as the nurse wheeled me down to the "holding" area. They dropped us off in a large room filled with people in wheel chairs that were obviously on their way home, as well. David pulled up, we loaded up and the kids trailed behind us as we pulled away from the Clinic and weaved our way back through Cleveland to head home.

David and I talked quite a bit on the way home and I was surprised how comfortable I was on the trip. The only thing that really bothered me was my nagging ache in my tail bone area, the nurses told me to get home and start eating and drinking my protein drink so that I would not develop a pressure ulcer there.

We were on the road for about thirty minutes when I called my mom and requested food, I remembered Dr. Mahdi's words earlier that day, I have to eat! I ordered baked chicken, mashed potatoes, her freezer corn, rolls and brownies; of course, she generously and graciously offered to have it all prepared when we arrived at home.

We were almost home and we started to see the dreaded orange construction signs, sure enough, 10 miles from our exit, traffic was at a complete stand still! I remember David being very frustrated and feeling so badly that he could not get me home any sooner. I was highly irritated at first, then I looked around at the clear blue sky, felt the extra warm sunshine on my face and thought, "Wow, I am so blessed!"

I remember riding up to my parents' home and pulling in the driveway, my stomach started feeling some happy butterflies, something I had not felt in quite a while! David came around and helped me out of the car, we walked into the garage and I could all ready smell the familiar scent of Mom's famous cooking. Mom and Pops greeted us as we walked into the kitchen, Mom came over and kissed me on the cheek, I looked over at the stove and saw all the items I had requested cooking on the stove and I realized again… there is NO place like home!

NINE

THE ROAD TO RECOVERY

There is nothing more frustrating to me when I am driving on a trip and my GPS assumes I have taken an incorrect path and the all familiar voice from my phone says, "recalculating!" Most times I have NOT taken a wrong turn, it just thinks I have, but, if I am trusting this device to guide me to my destination, I have to listen to it!

Being home and starting down the winding road to recovery was a definite time of recalculating in my life and I could sense that it was going to take daily prayer and motivation to train my mind to follow my new path.

Part of my recalculations began with not being able to sleep through the night, I would wake up at least two or three times and need to use the restroom. I do drink a good amount of water throughout the day, but getting up that much was highly frustrating, especially because I could not push the foot of the recliner down with my own strength, thus, Leisha had to wake up when I did to assist in my getting up and down process. In retrospect, I think I was getting up that much because my bladder and kidney had been "disturbed" during surgery and they also needed time to heal as did several other organs!

My incision was the size of Texas, not really, but close! The tightness from my incision made each task a bit more difficult because my core was so stiff and sore that I did not stand up straight and moving came very slowly. What was a day like in my recovery process? I am so glad you asked! Here is a sample of a daily schedule:

Wake up 8-8:30 a.m.

Devotions.

Breakfast which typically included French toast or pancakes, sometimes cooked apples and often a fried egg! (My mom is the best short order chef around!)

Rest in my recliner until around 10:00 a.m.

Walk laps in the house, started at five minutes, and kept going until I was walking for approximately 10-15 minutes at a time.

Use my incentive spirometer.

Get dressed, wash up, and even put on make up!

Rest in my recliner and watch HGTV or the Food Network (the Food Network kept me thinking of new things to eat and helped my appetite!)

Lunch, which consisted of left-overs or hotdogs, homemade mac and cheese, chicken nuggets from McDonalds, etc... typically topped off with a homemade brownie and Cool Whip

Rest in my recliner and watch the Food Network again.

Walk laps in the house.

Incentive Spirometer.

Drink my Boost at 2:00 p.m.

Walk laps in the house.

Rest in my recliner.

Supper.

Rest in my recliner.

Walk laps in the house.

Incentive Spirometer.

Evening snack which typically was a biscuit or toast.

Now, before any of you start judging my fattening and unhealthy eating habits … let me tell you what the nutritionist and Dr. Mahdi explained to me before I left the hospital! They informed me at Cleveland Clinic that my diet had to be GI-friendly, which basically means, everything fattening! Since Dr. Mahdi had performed bowel surgery on me, my bowel needed time to heal, so I had to eat things that were easily processed. Foods and items that were good for me to eat were fruit cups, sugars, baked goods, mashed potatoes, pasta, margarine NOT butter, vegetables that were cooked to death, meat cooked until it was more than fork tender, I could go on, but I think you get the picture.

According to the nutritionist, I was to stay on this diet until I started chemotherapy, perhaps longer! Well, I have to say that it was the most fun diet I have ever been on, I actually enjoyed it! ☺ Calories were very important for me as well, I needed to gain weight!

One of the complications that I had following my hospital stay was something I alluded to earlier, my sore tail bone! The first day that my friend Sara came to administer my Lovenox shot, we told her about how sore it was and she graciously went above and beyond and volunteered to check out the sore area for me! Not very many friends offer to check out a sore rear end, I knew we were going to end up like sisters through this one!

Sara checked it out and said I needed to take care of it right away because it was a large lesion and it was extremely enflamed. We contacted my family physician who suggested some large adhesive pads to wear over the wound to keep it clean and to help it heal. In addition, I sat on a rubber donut to take the pressure off my tailbone. I have to say that until I realized that Boost was an important part of my healing and could help heal this very uncomfortable area, it was a total struggle to try to drink it! My Boost tip of the day, drink it icy cold and poured over an overabundance of crushed, not cubed, ice! I did end up enjoying it and it is a great part of recovery and gaining strength back immediately following cancer diagnosis and surgery.

We could not believe how quickly the days seemed to pass and before we knew it we were on our way back to Cleveland to the brand-new Cancer Center and our meeting with Dr. Mahdi. David drove Mom and I to the appointment, his van was my very own limousine!

Walking to the elevators and back to Dr. Mahdi's offices seemed to be the longest walk ever since I was not accustomed to walking more than laps in the warm confines of my parent's home. David stayed in the waiting area and Mom went back with me for this momentous day!

We met with Dr. Mahdi's nurse first and she fielded my questions and concerns and explained that she would be the one to take out my thirty-four staples! Dr. Mahdi came in next, it was so great to see him, he just has such a comforting and encouraging way about him. He looked at my incision and said it was healing beautifully, checked out my sore bottom and said it was slowly on the mend as well. He was very proud that I had gained one or two pounds and praised me for my eating habits.

Dr. Mahdi then directed the conversation towards our next BIG step, chemotherapy. The two drugs I would be taking were Carboplatin and Taxol. He explained that I would be looking at chemo in "cycles", 1 cycle = 3 weeks. The first week of the therapy I would have both drugs, the second and third weeks I would have Taxol only. The list of side effects and what COULD happen was very lengthy, but he tried to be vague and leave it to the fact that each person responds differently.

Dr. Mahdi said his good-byes to us, hugged me and once again reassured me that I was "doing terrific, my dear!" Then, Jennifer came back in the room again. She had a large "staple remover" in her hand, it legitimately looked like an over-sized staple remover like I used in the office! She told me that during the removal procedure that if it became too much for me to handle she would gladly take a break since I had so many staples!

We chatted through the entire procedure and before long I looked down and she was over half way finished! I was so relieved that my staples coming out merely stung and it was uneventful. As I look back on it, I had surmised in my mind that after the staples came out I would be in less pain and be less stiff and sore … NOT TRUE! In place of the staples were very tight steristrips that had to fall off on their own.

After the appointment concluded and Mom and I had to walk back to the waiting area, I remember being very disappointed that I was still so tight, stiff and sore. I also remember walking down that hallway and thinking "Wow, this is the next enormous step in my journey! I must stay #initttowinit!"

We met up with David, he listened intently to the results of the appointment and even took a peak at my now staple-less incision! Then it was time to go back out in the cold and head down the very familiar twists and turns of downtown Cleveland to head home once again.

My recovery was not merely eating, sleeping, walking, resting and watching the Food Network! We had so many visitors throughout the recovery road. One visitor, in particular, was my co-worker, Chad. He came to visit me that week after I had my appointment with the good doc. It was so nice to see Chad, it was a little bit of normalcy to see his face and hear his up-lifting and positive voice again. One thing that stuck with Mom and I from our visit with Chad was his famous line as he was getting ready to leave. He said, "Lynn, I know it is difficult for you to eat, but you MUST gain strength to conquer this next step (he was referring to chemo)so, every time you finish a snack or a meal and you feel like you are completely full, eat two more bites for me!"

My Mom was so choked up from his concern for me that each time she would try to tell other people what he said to me she would well up with tears. Chad's positive and fun way of encouraging me ended up being one of the major influences outside of our family that helped get me through the roughest days!

The road to recovery was certainly going to be a long and winding one, but, it was this road less traveled that was made for me to follow. The truth that God was not surprised helped me through each daily struggle when I just could not see the end or started to question why. Recalculating is no longer frustrating to me, instead it is revitalizing and renews my perspective daily, it allows me opportunities I might have never encountered on the routine route. One thing is for certain, Chad's comment has never left me, I still catch myself eating those "two more bites!"

TEN

THE SILVER LINING

Recovery kept getting closer and closer as each day passed, each baby step resulted in another baby step and so forth. My appetite was finally getting to a new "normal" which I had not had in almost a year, food tasted good again, I did not get "full" in five minutes, I was able to eat an entire meal! I had gained a few pounds which was also a great sign for me and all of this leading up to the next hurdle, chemotherapy!

As I have mentioned, I had such terrific visits with family and friends, some folks traveled hundreds of miles to make a point to see me. Those visits meant more to me than I could express in this book. The visits, texts, Facebook posts, calls, packages, cards and mostly the PRAYERS are what brought me through so many rocky spots on my journey. Again, there are not adequate words to express the sincere appreciation I felt and continue to feel in my heart.

In the midst of my recovery from surgery, a dear friend, Stacy, purchased #inittowinit bracelets for me. Little did she know, or any of us for that matter, what an impact these purple and white bracelets would have on so many. The bracelets were very noticeable in their very deep purple color and then bright white writing, on one side was inscribed #itittowinit and on the other side, a cross and Philippians 4:13, my favorite verse. Stacy let me know that she had 1,200 bracelets, I remember thinking that was too many bracelets, I certainly would never run out of those!

April 18th 2017 finally arrived, the day of my first chemotherapy treatment! My lifelong friend, who I referred to earlier, Mary, came up as a surprise to go with us. She had already been such a help because she had gone through breast cancer several years earlier, she had been through it all, including chemo! Her knowledge and experience were such an amazing help to me and her presence for this crucial day was just icing on the cake.

My Mom, Leisha, Mary and I headed out to the Northcoast Cancer Center in Sandusky, Ohio early that Tuesday morning, I had to get lab work before my treatment and my appointment was at 9:00. Leisha drove us and we all talked and sang and laughed on the way to the appointment, it was a good distraction as I was more than anxious about this next step.

I had envisioned a hospital room when imagining what my chemotherapy treatment center might look like. We walked in to the lobby area and it was spacious and had an abundance of natural light, room for entertaining … sorry, just had to throw that HGTV reference in there!

A very nice lab nurse came out and called my name and I went back with her to the lab. She asked about our purple #inittowinit t-shirts, Mom, Mary and I wore them that day. I explained the whole meaning to her, it was so refreshing to see people's responses to our shirts and bracelets. The nurse took four vials of blood which was typically what happened when I had blood drawn. When she was finished I had to go back to the waiting area and wait for my designated time for chemo.

As we were sitting in the lobby waiting, I was extremely nervous, I had no idea what to expect or what this experience was going to be like, a complete unknown. I remember reciting my verse over and over in my mind, "I can do ALL things through Christ who strengthen me", ALL things. Leisha decided to take a selfie and little did we know that would be an activity that we would repeat at each and every chemo day!

A nurse finally came out and called us back, my entourage and I walked back through the hallway and entered the chemotherapy area. To my complete surprise, it was a beautiful, busy and friendly room, complete with walls made of windows! The windows overlooked a gorgeous courtyard with two water fountains and very lovely landscaping as well.

The room had places for twenty-one patients, plus two private rooms. We headed to the private "suite" which had places for everyone to sit, a TV for our viewing pleasure, as well as windows to look out at the rest of the room. My chair, as well as every chemo patient's chair is a very comfortable reclining chair and each patient space is equipped with a TV, how cool is that?

We had only been in our "private chemo suite" for a few minutes when a nurse walked in, she had a beaming smile and a personality to match. She introduced herself, she was Lynn, too, I had never met another Lynn! First, she wanted to know how much we knew about chemotherapy, Mary knew quite a bit from her own experience, but the rest of us were clueless.

Lynn went on to explain my chemo cocktail which was a combination of Carboplatin and Taxol. She explained in great detail the effects that the drugs could have on me and the bad reactions which could occur. People have more reactions to Taxol on their first visit than Carbo, so she told us to watch for side effects which would need addressed ASAP, such as, feeling very hot, light headed, and breathing difficulties. The good thing is that these symptoms typically show up within the first ten minutes of the drug going in, so, we would know right away if I was going to have issues.

Leisha had her Grace Community Church (our church) t-shirt on. Lynn saw it and commented that she attended church there as well! We were so excited that we had this in common and little did we know that this would only be the beginning of an amazing friendship with an amazing lady!

Lynn took great pains to explain each intricate detail of chemotherapy to us because she noted that once she administered the Benadryl to me I would be "out" for quite a while. She explained the pre-medications to me, I would be given Pepcid (antacid), Benadryl, Zofran (anti-nausea medication) and Decadron (a steroid) via my IV, all of this before the actual chemo drips started!

So, after her informative explanations, my first week of my first cycle was under way! Lynn put all of the pre-meds in through my IV and I remember the first effects of the Benadryl, WHOA, I felt it fast! I felt light headed and amazingly relaxed immediately, but not enough to make me fall asleep. She came back in after a few minutes and looked at me and said, "How are you still awake?" We laughed and I said that I was too nosy to fall asleep, I guess that was accurate.

I will never forget Lynn coming back in after she had looked at her computer for a long time, she was just astonished by all that I had been through! She came rushing in our room and said how sorry she was for all that had taken place and that she was shocked at how well I was doing after reading all that Dr. Mahdi had to do in surgery. I showed her my incision and again she was very surprised how great it looked and how well I was moving around. All of this was such an encouragement to me because I was discouraged thinking that I should have been doing much better than I was.

The pre-meds were finished and it was now time for the actual chemotherapy to begin. Taxol was up first, a one hour drip, I was so relieved after watching the first ten minutes tick away and realize that

I was not going to have the awful reactions she had explained to us in the beginning. Leisha felt comfortable enough to leave and drive to the nearest McDonalds and pick up lunch for my support team. I was so happy they could eat and relax in the room with me.

Next up, Carbo! That was only a thirty minute drip.

After it was all said and done, we had spent about five hours at the cancer center. I still remember the feeling of relief that I had survived my very first chemo treatment with no complications or bad reactions! Throughout the entire treatment we were getting to know Lynn more and more and before we left our "suite" I quietly asked her if I could request her again the next week. She reassured me in her kind and generous tone that she would be my nurse next week, too!

As we all left together that afternoon and headed home, I thanked God that He had seen me through yet another step along our journey. He is so faithful; my weakness shows off His strength and He is always the same even when my faith waivers... which was more often than I want to admit!

We got home from the Cancer Center and I was so thrilled with how I felt, I asked Leisha to go on a walk with me while Mom cooked supper. We walked all the way down our street and back, the farthest I had made it since surgery! I felt more energetic than I had in so long and I was so thrilled thinking that I was just going to be bigger than these treatments!

I ate well and felt pretty good the day following chemo and again I was so surprised that I was doing so well. Then Thursday hit, I woke up feeling muscle aches every place that I had a muscle. My head felt medicated, that is the only way to explain it and I was very weak. To my surprise, I was able to eat every meal and snack and was not nauseated even a tiny bit! Saturday came and I felt somewhat better, even better on Sunday and by Monday I was convinced that chemotherapy was NOT going to be that bad!

When the next chemo Tuesday came around I felt strong and ready to tackle week #2! Mom, Leisha and I walked into chemo, took our selfie and there was Lynn, ready to take care of me again. We had so much fun with her on this appointment and she meshed with all of us like we had known her all of our lives.

I gave Lynn one of my bracelets and she immediately put it on and said she would wear it always. Little did I know that she was serious! The nurses there referred to me as "the purple girl" because of my #inittowinit t-shirt which became my chemo uniform.

We finished up our appointment, hugged Lynn and headed out to our car to drive home and I was so thankful that week #2 was in the books. I noticed the deep blue sky, the billowing white, puffy clouds, felt the warm sunshine on my face and realized that nothing looked the same anymore. I was now living life in High Definition and I loved my new view.

I also realized on the way home that meeting Lynn was such a blessing, her friendship was already a gift that I knew I was going to cherish. Each experience we encounter in this life, whether happy or horrible, has a silver lining and Lynn was truly that, my silver lining!

#grateful

ELEVEN

FIRST IMPRESSIONS

The first few weeks of chemotherapy were pretty uneventful and I was feeling pretty good about this new "friend" of mine, chemotherapy! I realized my extreme need for it and it was treating me pretty nicely for a while. I had aches, muscle soreness, and fatigue, but I could deal with all of those and I was especially grateful that I had not experienced any nausea!

When my second cycle of chemo started, everything changed with this so-called friend of mine … chemo was no longer what he had appeared to be. I had my 2nd double dose, Carbo and Taxol, wow, it hit me hard this time! Thursday seemed to be the day that took a bad turn for me each week. This week was worse than any prior to it, nauseated, not hungry, my whole body hurt so badly, and my head felt like a brick had hit me square on the forehead!

I remember asking Lynn about it the first time, if it was supposed to be this rough and she explained to me that as chemo builds up in your system, it continues to get a bit more difficult with each treatment. I always went to Lynn for the truth because her knowledge and experience are invaluable, and she is straight forward, no beating around the bush, it helped prepare me for what would come next.

I can tell you that after that 2nd double dose, I realized that I was no longer kicking chemo's butt, it was now kicking mine with a vengeance! I mentioned that I received Zofran in my pre-med's each week, that was no longer doing the trick, I had to start taking it at home on Thursday as well. I would typically take anti-nausea medication on Thursday and Friday at least. Lynn requested an additional nausea medicine for me to take during pre-meds. This medicine stayed in my system for three days and added another thirty-minutes to my chemo day. It helped, and it was well worth the extra time.

I remember the first time that I started getting really nauseated, it was late on Friday afternoon and I was so discouraged because I felt like I should be feeling better by Friday … NOT ANY MORE! When the nausea progressed to its worst point, I would dry heave, that was probably my least favorite thing.

Coupling the nausea with not eating or drinking very much, I would feel so extremely weak by Saturday. I remember getting up to go to the bathroom or even considering getting out of my pajamas becoming such chores that unless it was a necessity, I just stayed in my chair. My mom was always there with me and would offer me different things to eat or drink and I would graciously decline because I just knew that I could not put anything in my stomach.

The above scenario was true of week one of each cycle when I received both drugs. Weeks two and three when I was only given Taxol, it was not as severe. I could typically eat well throughout those weeks and the main side effects were weakness, headache, body aches and fatigue.

Looking back, the most frustrating thing was that by the time I was feeling half way "human" again, it was time to head back for more chemo! Someone asked me the other day if I had one piece of advice for someone recently diagnosed with cancer and chemotherapy, what would it be? I thought about that for a long time and my response was "make sure you have your person or people you can go to when you want to give up because there will be quitting spots every single day, but you can't, you have to have down 'moments' but not days or weeks. All of your energy has to be focused on getting well and beating this thing, break downs take way too much of your strength!"

I have always heard that first impressions can be deceiving, that was never so true to me as it was with chemo! It starts out pretty mild and makes you think you are stronger and that this will not be "that bad". Then it fights back like nothing you have ever seen and when that happens, what do you do? You fight HARDER, you CAN'T GIVE UP and you realize that it is a necessary evil to aid you in reaching your goal of being cancer free! Chemotherapy is a temporary hell, but the key word is TEMPORARY, you just have to last longer than it does!

Bottom line is, I can't like chemo ... no one can, but I can't like cancer more!

TWELVE

CELEBRATIONS AND SURPRISES

Chapter 12 is going to be different than the rest, the look, the feel, and the whole deal. I am creating it to be different because I want it to be a gallery of summaries of celebrations and surprises that took place during my chemo season. So... please, sit back, relax and enjoy these celebrations and surprises with me!

Ovarian Sisterhood

My second week of chemo, Mom, Leisha and I were there, talking and taking selfies and doing what we did each week ... all of a sudden someone walked into the treatment area that totally caught Mom off guard. I remember her being engaged in our conversation one minute and then the next she had a complete distraction! She looked at us and said, "Is that Patti Tucker?" Patti had been Mom's hair stylist when I was very young, and I always remembered her because of her big heart, smile and personality, just a great lady!

Finally, Mom stood up to take a closer look, sure enough, it was Patti. I remember Mom looking so sad, she was so shocked at how sick Patti looked. Mom decided to get up and go over to her. Patti was so happy to see Mom and explained that she had recently been diagnosed with, you guessed it, Ovarian Cancer! Mom told her about me and Patti got right up and came over and grabbed my hand and talked to me like we were best friends.

Patti and I exchanged brief summaries of our stories and found out we had the exact same diagnosis, surgery, incision, doctor and chemo schedule! From that moment, we shared a bond, a bond that cannot be broken! We text, we talk, we have cried, laughed and shared each moment of our journey with each other. We are now "sisters" and I am so thankful for our friendship.

During chemo, I started writing a blog, it was very therapeutic for me to say the least. My hope was that my experiences, feelings and writing would help someone else who was going through a struggle of any kind, but especially, cancer.

Someone saw my blog via Facebook and told their mother in law about it because she had been recently diagnosed with Ovarian cancer. Through a series of events, I found out that this person was named Kim, a lady that we had known 30 years prior because we had her children in our daycare center that my Mom administrated. Long story short, Kim and I found each other and sure enough, she had a similar diagnosis to us and was going through surgery and going to be on the same chemo regimen as Patti and I!

Kim and I talked quite a few times before her surgery and then through her recovery process. Once her chemo started up, Patti and Kim connected as well. We have all been knit together through each one of our journeys. Kim's friends and family had a huge fund raiser and benefit for her, a chicken dinner, Patti and her family, me and my family and Sara's family all met there that day to rally around Kim and support her. When Kim walked into the room that day, the love for her was so immense and Patti and I were thrilled and honored to be on the front row cheering her on!

One thing is for certain, our Ovarian Sisterhood has helped and encouraged all three of us and I know that we will all be bonded together for life! #ovariansistersare4ever

Viral Bracelets

Remember that I mentioned the bracelets that Stacy ordered for us and that she ordered 1,200 of them? What I had not mentioned until now is the fact that these purple bands went viral! All from word of mouth and Facebook, friends, family, acquaintances and complete strangers started ordering them!

I made them available by donation, no set price, the goal was not to profit from them, but rather to encourage people with the meaning behind them. I took on the bracelet orders and distribution because I needed an outlet, something to make me feel like I was still a contributor in some way.

One by one, I would go down to Grund Drug Store in Fremont, they have a full-service post office in their store which is where I mailed out the bracelets. Sometimes I would go down there daily, sometimes a couple times per week, but always to mail these packages of bracelets.

The clerk who assisted me each time finally asked me what I was mailing in the packages, I explained about my cancer and the bracelets of hope and strength. She loved the entire story and talked to the owner of the store and they offered to place my bracelets in their store so that their customers could donate and purchase them. We were so taken back by their generous offer.

Each week when I visited their post office I would also pick up the donations from the bracelets, by the time the bracelets were gone, they had collected over $600! These were mostly purchased by total strangers who read my story and wanted to help or just wanted the bracelet! I will never forget Grund Drug for their generosity, support and encouragement through the bracelets.

At the time that I am writing this we have distributed over 1,200 bracelets to at least 23 states and Spain! We have had so many stories of folks enduring cancer that have requested the #inittowinit bands and somehow the band reminded them to keep going and not give up.

There was an older man in Tennessee who had cancer and had been given a bracelet by my aunt, he loved it and wore it every day. Unfortunately, this gentleman passed away, my uncle and aunt went to the funeral home and when they walked up to his casket, his family had placed that purple bracelet in between his hands. It is so humbling and awesome that God has used my bracelets to encourage people all over the country no matter what struggle they were facing.

The Wedding

I was so happy when we met with Dr. Mahdi in May and he let me know that he was fine with me postponing one week of chemotherapy so that I would be a bit stronger for Leisha and Tim's wedding on May 27th! I cannot explain how happy I was to know that I would be at least be strong enough to enjoy the festivities and soak up each moment of my daughter's wedding day.

Friday, May 26th I was able to go to the reception hall and assist in decorating. I really only wrote on signs and things like that, but they made me feel like I was truly helping. Mary was here to lead in decorating the hall, she truly did magic in that room for us.

The wedding site was in the most beautiful gardens, outside; thus, good weather was a must. We did not rent a tent because we were trusting that the ominous forecast was wrong and that the weather would be perfect for their big day! The rehearsal started off with raindrops, but we carried on with the program ignoring the rain completely!

After the rehearsal, we went back to a hotel and had the rehearsal dinner, Chris so graciously offered to have the dinner all set up upon our arrival and she did. We had approximately fifty people in the rehearsal dinner area, all family and close friends, it was so nice. I got up and thanked everyone for coming and helping and let them know how thankful I was to be a part of the weekend and thanked everyone for prayers. There were tears, but only briefly, we were there to have a good time!

We all spent the night there, almost the entire bridal party and other close friends and family. Chris and I stayed in a room together, her goal was to keep me calm until the big day! We laughed, laughed, and laughed some more, even the bride to be and a couple of her bridesmaids came in our room for a while.

One of my favorite things about Chris is how we can talk about literally EVERYTHING. I remember asking her a question that had been weighing on my mind for quite some time, I said, "Chris, if you knew way back when that I would end up with advanced cancer like this, would you still want us to be best friends?" She did not even hesitate before she answered that she would not change a thing. I am so blessed with the best family in the entire world and then friends like Chris. #mysupportteamisthebest

The morning of the wedding was upon us and we all woke up very early to begin the festivities! The weather had cleared up and it was gorgeous outside, we were relieved and grateful for that. I remember feeling so tired that morning, but more thankful than tired, I was healthy enough to be at my kid's wedding!

My friend Terri had so graciously accepted the duties of being Leisha and Tim's wedding coordinator and she did a masterful job that day! I recall standing outside of a little cottage where I had been hiding in the air conditioning for the hour before the ceremony and I saw my son walking back to escort me up to the ceremony sight. All of the sudden, Celine Dion's *Because You Loved Me* started playing as the background for the parents to be seated, the flood gates that had been locked up finally opened!

Luke took my arm in his and said, "Momma, you have to pull it together!" He chuckled at me being so emotional and did his best to make me laugh, it was not working. It was like all of the emotions I had held in for the past few months all decided to leak out in one fail swoop! I noticed as we walked through the sea of people in the audience that several people were shedding tears as we walked down, so at least I was not alone.

As I stood in honor of my daughter coming down the winding stairway in her magnificent gown, I looked up and saw her Dad escorting her and I remembered her as a little girl saying that all she wanted to do was be able to walk down stairs in her wedding gown someday. Her someday had come! She looked flawless and the entire day followed suit, it was a nearly flawless day.

The reception was absolutely like something out of magazine, Mary had out done herself making it into the blingy and glamorous party that Leisha had always dreamed of. We had so much fun, made so many memories and I was never so happy to step onto the dance floor to have our Mother-Daughter dance. We danced to the theme song for Gilmore Girls, Where You Lead, I will Follow… perfect for us as we are a bit obsessed with the series.

At the end of the day when I had to leave the reception because I was so tired, I just could not help but thank God over and over for the honor and privilege to be a part of this day. #leishaandtimchism

Surprises

The Pink Heals Tour came through our area the summer of my chemo. It is a people's charity that volunteers to come to visit very sick people with varying diseases, not just cancer, they come on a pink firetruck! My cousin had given them my name and they came to visit us at my parent's home. The firetrucks came up with sirens blaring, our local fire department accompanied the Pink Heals truck.

They came to the door with flowers and lots of hugs and I was invited to come out and sign their Pink Heals truck, I was overwhelmed by the gesture and by all of the hundreds of signatures already on the truck. One of the really amazing things was that Lissa Guyton from 13 ABC News in Toledo came out to cover our story and the Pink Heals Tour! It was almost surreal to come out the door and see the trucks, as well as the 13 ABC News camera in our front yard!

The Shoe

My birthday is July 16th and this birthday was particularly special, not only was I actually HERE for it, but I was also turning 50! Luke and Leisha gave me a date to set aside because they had a big surprise for me! I gladly held the date open and prayed that I would feel up to whatever they had planned for me.

We went to my great nephew Brody's birthday party and then I headed out with Luke, Ali, Leisha and Tim, I had no idea what our destination was! We headed south and that could have lead us so many places that I still had no clue where we were going. We stopped off at a Five Guys to eat on the way, one of my favorite food destinations! They ended up taking me to a hotel in Columbus and they said we were stopping there on our way to my ultimate birthday surprise destination!

The next morning, we got up and got ready, they had given me a birthday present early, a new Ohio State t-shirt! After we were all ready for the day they walked me to the car then instructed me to close my eyes for the drive to our surprise location. I followed my orders and it was not a very long drive and we had arrived!

I was given MORE instructions to follow, I had to keep my eyes closed while they pushed me in my wheel chair to the mystery place.

Again, I followed my instructions and did not even peak as we moved swiftly towards wherever we were going!

When my wheel chair stopped, they told me to look up... I hesitantly opened my eyes and in front of me was The Ohio State Buckeyes stadium, we were at "The Shoe"! The kids had arranged a private tour of the stadium! I was so excited I cried, as we went on the very amazing tour, we took pics and made memories along the way. We got to go through the tunnel that the Buckeyes run out at each home game, as we entered the tunnel, I was overcome with emotions and cried again!

As we concluded the tour on the Block O in the middle of the football field, we took many pictures and I was overwhelmed with gratitude that my kids would have taken the time to plan the absolute perfect birthday present for me! My 50th birthday was definitely one for the record books, I will cherish that day for always!

#ihavethebestkids

My 50th

My birthday was such an amazingly fun celebration this year! It was funny to think back to the beginning of 2017 when I thought the biggest things I would face this year would be turning 50 and maybe going through the change! Ha!

The day before my birthday we planned for a bunch of my closest friends, my nieces and sister to go to lunch to celebrate at Margaritaville. We had an amazing group that day, friends I have known my whole life to newer friends, it was absolutely incredible! One of my favorite parts of the day was taking a group photo in front of the waterfall outside the restaurant, it is a picture that I will treasure always.

On my actual birthday, my parents planned for us to go to Ole' Zim's, one of my favorite family style restaurants in this area. We had an amazing meal and I actually felt like eating.

Combine these festivities with the cards and gifts I received and it was without a doubt, the best birthday I have ever had. I am truly thankful for my memories of turning the big 5-0!

Christmas in July

My friend Eunice is one of those friends who has been there throughout my entire life. She is more like a sister than just a friend. Eunice, my mom and my friend Terri, all got together and decided to surprise me with a Christmas in July party after my birthday celebrations had ceased. I thought Mom and I were just going to her house for lunch, instead there were Christmas decorations everywhere, delicious food, a Christmas tree and Christmas presents!

It was an amazingly thoughtful gesture and I am so thankful that I had another great diversion from chemo that involved my absolute favorite holiday just a tad bit early!

#Christmasinjulyrocks

I realize this "chapter" was a bit lengthy, but, I hope that you enjoyed this gallery of some of my favorite surprises and celebrations. One thing is for certain, each moment and memory mean just a little bit more and I have never been more thankful for each relationship in my life. #myheartishappy

THIRTEEN

FOREVER GRATEFUL

I remember getting to the mid-way point of chemotherapy and thinking that I just could not finish it. I could not see the end and even with all of the delightful diversions my family and friends were granting me with, I just did not think I could get through the final three cycles.

My friend Sara and I were talking one evening and she mentioned that if I wanted to have a big celebration when chemo was over that we could have it at her house. I brushed it off because I was just not in the mood to even think about it, would I even make it through to the end?

A few days later I was thinking about our conversation and finally it hit me what a terrific idea this was! I needed a final goal, something to keep me focused and determined to make it through! Let's have a celebration!

Sara and I talked it over, chose a date in September and started making the arrangements. I was so excited because she was actually having a pig roast and she told me to invite as many family and friends as I wanted to have!

We invited over one hundred people and I called this party my "Forever Grateful" party. I absolutely could not wait to get all of these special people gathered together for a day of thanks and celebrating, it definitely kept me going!

After my fifth double dose of chemo, I bottomed out. My counts dropped, my strength had vanished and I did not bounce back from the side effects. I talked to Lynn and she assured me that it was okay to postpone chemo in hopes that the week off would give me the strength to finish strong. I did bounce back a bit better after taking the week off and the rest from chemo was apparently just what I needed.

After my final double dose, Leisha told me that if I was too weak and tired to go back for chemo the next week, she was going to CARRY me there! We laughed about that scenario and it helped me gain my determination back again! I think just knowing it was almost over kept me motivated to push on because I seemed to rebound more quickly than ever during that last cycle ... I could finally see the end!

My last chemo treatment was scheduled for August 29th, to my surprise, my Uncle Bill and Aunt Charlene were visiting from Tennessee and they wanted to meet us there for the big event. (they brought my cousins, Alyssa and Caylin with them as well!)

Leisha, Mom and I headed out for my final treatment, we commented on the way that it looked like it might rain. I love rain and storms now, very ironic, because I was always afraid of storms before I had cancer. I made the statement several times during chemo that I would love to have a storm while we were there because of all the windows at the center, it would be so amazing to see a storm through those! It did rain once in 18 weeks, but that was all, no storms!

We arrived at the center just in time for my treatment, we met up with our family that was visiting there and our crew headed in!

Several of us had our purple t-shirts on, #inittowinit, it seemed appropriate!

Our biggest concern for this appointment was if my veins would hold up for one more week or not, the past 6 weeks had been touch and go where my veins were concerned. Dr. Mahdi did not order a port for me; thus, my veins had taken a severe beating!

We were able to have a private suite and it was a good thing with all of the people we had with us this time! Lynn came bounding over to be my nurse for this momentous day, I was so happy, it was only fitting to have her this last time. She made sure we were all situated before she came in with the bag of heat she placed on the best vein in my left arm to try to wake that vein up one more time!

She came back in a few minutes later to attempt the IV, she wanted it to work so badly, not as badly as I did! Lynn inserted it and had that look on her face, the look that we did not want to see! She made the comment that there was not blood return so she knew it was not working, we all started praying hard and after a few minutes of prodding and readjusting it, the vein started working! #relief

Leisha made her customary trip to McDonalds and it just seemed like a typical day at the center until I leaned back in the chair, relaxing with my Benadryl and realizing, we have made it, this is it!! I brought cards and candy for the nurses and a special gift for Lynn. I wanted to express my gratitude to these ladies who had become like family to us, they had taken such terrific care of me!

The next time Lynn poked her head in I asked her to come in because I had a gift for her, she expressed the fact that I did not need to do that, but finally came in and sat down beside me. She opened up her little black box, there was a shiny double heart necklace from Kay Jewelers. Lynn welled up with tears, so did I, what a journey we had all gone through together!

As the hours passed and the last bit of Taxol dripped into my IV, the time had finally come, my final chemo was finished! Patients that had become friends to me stopped in to congratulate me, the feeling of relief and gratitude were almost overwhelming!

We gave an abundance of hugs, thanks and "see ya later's" and then headed home. On the way home, I thanked God and made phone calls to immediate family to let them know the final treatment was finally over. I enjoyed my ride home more than I had the past 20 weeks and was thankful for every cloud, every tree that was starting to turn fall colors and just enjoyed each second!

I knew I had to get home and begin resting up for my next big day, that Friday, Luke was taking me for my final PET scan (CT Scan with Contrast), then the next Tuesday, September 5th, we would meet with Dr. Mahdi. So... I did just that, stayed at home, rested, ate and endured my final rough side effects from chemo!

Friday, September 1st, Luke picked me up and drove me to my final scan, for now! I always dread the CT scans because of the super-sized cocktail I have to drink before the scan can happen! Alas, I drank it all and my scan was complete! Luke and I headed to Berardi's, one of our favorite Sandusky restaurants, and enjoyed our time together and celebrating the final CT.

Now came the wait for Tuesday, September 5th, THE DAY we have been waiting for! Tim, Leisha and Mom escorted me to our results meeting with Dr. Mahdi. We sat in the exam room waiting for him. Finally, we heard his voice and there he was!

He came in the room, greeted all of us, asked how we were, and then slid over in front of the computer to find out results. First of all, my final C125 tumor marker was down to 27!! (0-39 is normal!) It was absolutely a miracle to us that I went down from almost 13,000 to 27, thank you, God! Then he discussed the scan ... the nodules on my lung are still there, not changed, he thinks the spots are benign and from pollutants, but we will keep an eye on those. There is a small spot on the stem to my liver which could be a tiny blood clot, again, we will keep an eye on that as well.

Finally, he said the words we had been waiting to hear for the past seven months... "Lynn, you are cancer free, my dear!" He had to end the appointment with my percentages which honestly, are not good. He hesitantly let us know that I have a 60-70% chance of a cancer recurrence pretty quickly. In Dr. Mahdi fashion, he followed that up with, "But, someone has to be in the 30% and my dear, I believe that will be you!" I WAS CANCER FREE!!!!!!

All of us let out a muffled cheer, he hugged us and said I would see him at our next appointment in a few months. I can remember walking down to the chemo center to let the nurses know the news, we had such a huge celebration with all of them!

As we walked out to our car Leisha had us stop and take another selfie, our last selfie at the Cancer Center, it is a picture I will always treasure! The relief and thankfulness was absolutely overwhelming and the drive home seemed sweeter than ever!

The Indians

I have always been a huge sports nut, I adore football and basketball and of course, as I have alluded to previously, I am an absolute Ohio State Buckeye fan to the core! That being said, I have never been a baseball fan, watching baseball on tv was like having needles poked in my eyes!

Throughout chemo, I had a change of heart, Pops always watched the Cleveland Indians and I found myself starting to enjoy the games ... sometimes I would catch myself watching the games even when he was not home! Yes, by the end of chemo, I was a full-fledge Indians fan! I knew the players, their positions, and even made my first Indians t-shirt purchase.

This leads up to a couple of amazing outings I was able to go on! My youth pastor when I was a Sophomore in high school, Pastor Jeff, is now the chaplain for the Detroit Tigers. The Tigers were coming to Cleveland to play the Indians and he had tickets for the game! He text me and asked if Sara, Luke and I would be interested in going to the game with he and his wife, Karla, we were more than willing to accept the invitation!

We had an absolute blast with them, I had not seen them in thirty years! We had seats ten rows up, right behind home plate, terrific seats! My son had tweeted out about us going to the game and that it was my first Indians game and that I had just beat cancer and they communicated with him and there was yet another surprise for me! A group of people from the stadium came up behind us during the game and announced that I had just been declared cancer free, everyone in our section cheered, they presented me with an array of Indians certificates, foam finger, and a certificate signed by the Indians owner!

The Indians won huge that night and we had a terrific time! I posted on Facebook about the game and a life-long friend, Tom, saw it. He did not realize that I liked baseball now and was so thrilled to hear that bit of news about me. He text me the next night and said he bought front row, field level, seats and wanted to take my Pops and me! So, a couple of weeks later, we headed out with Tom and his dad and were literally right on the field! We had another unforgettable night!

The Pig Roast … FOREVER GRATEFUL

September 9th rolled around and with it came a spectacularly beautiful Autumn day! There was a clear blue sky with passing puffy white marshmallow clouds, a brisk breeze and everything about it was perfect. We headed to Sara's house at the given time and I was shocked when I walked into their "garage"!

Their garage was transformed into a party hall complete with Buckeye decorations and a large variety of delicious food … and let us not forget the guest of honor, THE PIG! Sara walked me out to the pig roasting area and they graciously allowed me to have the first bite of pork, it was the most delicious pork I had ever tasted!

Family and friends started pouring in, I was literally astonished at how many people were there just to help celebrate our victory! Sara had a sign by the end of her long driveway that read, "Honk, Lynn is Cancer Free!" Everything was nothing short of perfect, the perfect day of celebration.

When it was time to eat, I stood in front of the 80ish people that were there and thanked them for their prayers, gave God the biggest praise and shed some happy tears. David prayed to bless the food and the eating commenced! The food was magnificent and being able to see that many people who are important and special to me in one place was like a dream come true, well worth the wait.

David had worked tirelessly on a DVD for the day that contained almost 300 pictures of the people and places of my journey. David had me pick out songs to back up these pictures and I chose songs that meant a lot to me and helped express my feelings that day. I watched the DVD several times before the event and I cried every single time, it was a the most fitting conglomeration of memories and moments!

At the end of the day, I could honestly say that the only statement that could possibly summarize my feelings was, "Forever Grateful!"

The Buckeye Game

Stacy bought Buckeyes tickets for Tim, Leisha and I, we were going to the football game vs Maryland, our first time to attend a Big Ten match up! We were so excited and counting down the days. We were so grateful for her generosity in giving us such an amazing gift.

There is an Ohio State personality who has become uncommonly popular, he is referred to as "The Big Nut". He goes to almost every single game, paints his face, wears his OSU garb and is typically on national TV during each Buckeye game. Stacy had arranged for us to go to his tailgate before the game, how cool! We attended Big Nut's festivities, took pictures with him and one of the best parts of the day was seeing him in a new t-shirt for the day … he wore a scarlet and gray, #inittowinit shirt, just for me! I was touched and honored beyond words!

We then headed to meet up with friends at the Skull Session, an Ohio State marching band concert that happens before each home game. We were able to see Urban Myer and the football team walk through, they were literally twenty feet from us!

Then came THE GAME, we were in our seats two hours early so that we did not miss a thing and we did not! Our seats were right beside the best damn band in the land and the student section, right on the end zone, absolutely phenomenal views! We enjoyed every second of a huge Buckeye victory! Of course, as with each of these events, the best part of the entire experience were the memories made.

This is NOT A Conclusion

Trying to close out this book is very difficult for me because this is NOT a conclusion! This is not the end to my story, nor my entire story, but, as I have been reminded of so many times throughout the past eight months, this was merely a chapter in my story.

Life is short, we have no guarantees of tomorrow, life can stop you on a dime, and the expressions can go on and on. One thing is certain, there are no certainties in this life. Larger than that truth is that we have a God who is ALWAYS certain, never changes and is never surprised. The God that saw me through each day, each trial and each victory is the same God who will be there for you, too, if you let Him in!

Enjoy each moment, embrace each memory, hug your family, say I love you to your special people and try to live each day in high definition … you will never regret it! Mostly, always have the #inittowinit mentality, no matter what you are facing! Finally, be forever grateful for the moments in this life that take your breath away and may each moment be worthy of that.

#FOREVER GRATEFUL … by the way, I still might ride a bull named Fu-Manchu!

EPILOGUE

DON'T PASS THE BALL

I know, you thought the book was finished! I was compelled to add this last sub-chapter and lately, whenever I feel compelled to do something, I do it!

Basketball was my main focus through high school, I did not just play the game for fun, I played it with a passion because I loved it! I studied the game, I practiced every day in my drive way. I remember from the time I was a Freshman in high school I would shoot 100 foul shots a day, no matter the weather, I was out in the driveway working on my form, follow through and to make sure I did NOT shoot like a girl!

My Senior year I had an invitation to play at one of our area private schools because I had attended their summer camp. I declined to take their offer because I was determined to finish my varsity career at Temple Christian Academy! David was my coach and we had a promising season ahead of us ... until right before the season. Four of my fellow class mates and team mates disregarded team rules and were suspended from our team for my entire senior season!

So, we embarked on the most important season of my basketball career with four JV players and myself. David arranged plays specifically for me and we were going forward with a positive mind set, this was my last season after all!

Extremely long story short, we went through our entire season undefeated heading into the championship game at our version of a State Tournament in Findlay, Ohio. We had faced this same team twice during the season and obviously had beaten them both times, so they were more than ready for us!

I remember like it was yesterday how the game went, the score was tied more times than in any other game we had played all season long. We were two points ahead with one minute left in regulation, David called his last time out. That huddle was so intense to my 17-year-old mind, the whole season, my whole career was on the line. David said, "Lynn, you bring the ball up and stall for as long as possible, they will have to foul you, DO NOT PASS THE BALL!"

We went back out on the floor and I brought the ball up, the second I crossed half court, Findlay had three girls waiting to converge on me. I could not dribble around them, they surrounded me like three giant walls! I looked down the court and one of my team mates was standing directly under our basket with no one within ten feet of her, finally, out of desperation and panic, I reached around one of the defenders and delivered a perfect bounce pass down to her. The ball hit her hands and flew out of bounds, we had lost the ball with less than a minute to go in the game!

The gym suddenly fell gravely quiet and while it was still and silent David yelled, "Lynn Case, if we lose this game by two points, it's your fault!" My heart sank, he was right, I did not follow his game plan, I panicked! Things happened quickly in the last minute and I had a last second shot to win the game and it rimmed the hoop and fell out, we lost the game 50-48!

I laid down on the court and did not want to get up. I was exhausted, every muscle hurt, I had played with a broken finger on my shooting hand and it was now throbbing. I scored all 48 of our points, the announcer was trying to present me with the Most Valuable Player of the tournament award and all I wanted to do was lay there and cry.

David walked over to me, reached out his hand to help me up, I very grudgingly stood up. I walked out and accepted the award and our team received our 2nd place trophy. After everything was finished and I was walking out of the locker room, there stood David. He walked over to me, put his arm around me and said, "You passed the ball". We both let out sarcastic chuckles and we walked out of the gym for the final time.

On the way home, I went over to David's seat on the bus and sat down, I looked at him and said, "I am so sorry that I passed the ball, I did not follow through with your game plan and I lost the game." Tears welled up again in my eyes and I felt so defeated. He accepted my apology and said that he should have never yelled what he did during the game, he was sorry, as well.

We have laughed many times about the happenings of this infamous game for the TCA Lady Warriors. Isn't it funny how perspective changes as time moves on and things that seemed so important really were not? David was the best coach that I ever had and he pushed me to be more than I probably should have been because he believed in me more than I believed in myself! At the end of the day, if I would have followed his simple instruction, we probably would have won that game!

I had told Chad about the above story in one of our hundreds of sports conversations we are so famous for. During chemotherapy, about nine weeks in, when I wanted to quit and thought I just could not go on anymore; I received a text from Chad, it simply said, "Don't Pass The Ball!"

He was gently reminding me that God had allowed me to go through cancer for a reason and He believed in me and knew that I could handle the pressure if I would just follow His game plan. This was MY experience, MY hurt and MY trial, I had to finish the game without panicking and without trying to pass the ball to someone else who was not prepared for it!

Whatever you face in your life, just remember that there is a reason it is you facing it, you are equipped to handle the giants that are surrounding you like walls! May the most difficult times we face in this life show off God's strength and may we believe in ourselves the way that He does and no matter what…

Don't Pass the Ball!

Made in the USA
Columbia, SC
06 December 2017